CYCLING'S
STRANGEST®
TALES

Other titles in the STRANGEST series

Cricket's Strangest Matches
Fishing's Strangest Tales
Football's Strangest Matches
Golf's Strangest Rounds
Horse Racing's Strangest Tales
Kent's Strangest Tales
Law's Strangest Cases
London's Strangest Tales
London's Truly Strangest Tales
Medicine's Strangest Cases
Motor Racing's Strangest Races
Rugby's Strangest Matches
Running's Strangest Tales
Shakespeare's Strangest Tales
Teachers' Strangest Tales
Tennis's Strangest Matches

Titles coming soon

Railways' Strangest Tales
Royalty's Strangest Tales

CYCLING'S STRANGEST TALES

Extraordinary but true stories
from over two hundred years of cycling

IAIN SPRAGG

PORTICO

First published in the United Kingdom in 2017 by
Portico
43 Great Ormond Street
London
WC1N 3HZ

An imprint of Pavilion Books Company Ltd

ISBN 978-1-91104-255-6

A CIP catalogue record for this book is available from the British Library.

10 9 8 7 6 5 4 3 2 1

Reproduction by Mission Productions Ltd, Hong Kong
Printed and bound by Bookwell, Finland

This book can be ordered direct from the publisher at www.pavilionbooks.com

CONTENTS

INTRODUCTION   11

THE FALSE PRETENDERS (1478)   14

FAME BUT NO FORTUNE FOR THE BARON (1818)   16

THE DANGERS OF PEDAL POWER (1839)   18

HOW TO AVOID A WATERY FALL AT THE WATERFALL (1869)   20

CHANNELLING THE POWER (1883)   23

THE AMAZING TRAVELS OF THOMAS (1884)   25

CYCLING'S DEBT TO STARLEY (1885)   28

THE TYRE WARS (1887)   31

THE WRIGHT STUFF (1892)   33

ANSWERING THE CALL OF NATURE (1893)   35

FRANK'S FATAL FORAY (1894)   37

ALL THAT GLITTERS IS NOT GOLD (1896)   39

THE HEART OF THE MATTER (1896)   41

THE LAST MADISON SQUARE MARATHON (1898)   43

NO PAIN, NO GAIN (1904)   45

THE TOUR'S EARLY TROUBLES (1904)   48

THE TOUR'S MYSTERY MAN (1904)   51

CHRISTOPHE BATTLES THE ELEMENTS (1910)   53

DUBOC'S WATER-BOTTLE WOE (1911)   55

DANGER IN THE DARKNESS (1912)   57

THE PELISSIER PROTEST (1924)   59

VICTOR DENIED VICTORY (1929)   61

THE BIG BINDA BRIBE (1930)   63

OLYMPIC SKULDUGGERY (1936)   65

WAR ON WHEELS (1937)   67

A YEAR IN THE SADDLE (1939)   69

THE BRAVERY OF BARTALI (1943)   72

TOEING THE LINE (1947)   74

CHICAGO DEFIES CONVENTION (1948)   76

BOYD'S BELGIAN BLUNDER (1950s)   78

UPROAR OVER OSCAR (1950s)   80

THE AUSSIES' UNLIKELY TANDEM TRIUMPH (1952)   82

AT ONE WITH NATURE (1954)   84

NOT A PRETTY PICTURE (1956)   86

UNBEATABLE BERYL (1959)   88

AU REVOIR, MONSIEUR LE PRESIDENT (1960)   90

CYCLING ON THE CURRICULUM (1961)   92

THE IDIOCY OF INERTIA (1965)   94

THE WHITE BIKE MAN (1965)   96

OUT OF THIS WORLD (1973)   98

BMX GETS A 'BUM' DEAL (1974)   100

LUCK OF THE IRISH RUNS OUT (1975)   102

THE BREAKAWAY THAT BACKFIRED (1978)   104

THE MARVEL OF MUNI (1980s)   106

HOY'S DEBT TO HOLLYWOOD (1982)   108

MORGAN'S BEASTLY LEAP (1982)   110

INTO THE VALLEY OF DEATH (1983)   112

THE GREAT GLOBAL DASH (1984)   114

'LOOK, NO HANDS!' (1985)   117

ONWARD CHRISTIAN SOLOIST (1988)   119

'ST MICHAEL' TO THE RESCUE (1990)   121

MARIO AND THE PIN-UP (1990s)   123

STAIRWAY TO HEAVEN (1993)   126

THE CRASH-TEST COPPER (1994)   127

WOMEN, WHEELS & POLITICS (1996)   129

TWO WHEELS VERSUS FOUR LEGS (1997)   131

AN UNLIKELY MEDICAL HERO (2000)   133

LAURA'S LEARNING CURVE (2000)   135

SIR BRADLEY'S VEGETARIAN PORKIES (2001)   137

MANSER'S AFRICAN ODYSSEY (2003)   139

HORSES FOR COURSES (2003)   141

THE NUMBERS GAME (2004)   143

MUDDYING THE WATERS (2005)   145

THE FOLD-AWAY PHENOMENON (2006)   147

WHO LET THE DOGS OUT? (2007)   149

THE LOVE THAT DARE NOT SPEAK ITS NAME (2007)   151

YOU'VE BEEN FRAMED (2007)   153

PLUMBING NEW DEPTHS (2008)   155

THE MADNESS OF SIR DAVE (2008)   157

AIN'T NO SUNSHINE ANY MORE (2008)   159

GOING FOR GOLD (2008)   161

COPENHAGEN'S CONGESTED CLAIM TO FAME (2008)   163

RISING TO THE OCCASION (2008)   165

THE SUMMIT OF CYCLING (2009)   167

BOBBIES ON BIKES (2009)   169

IT'LL ALL COME OUT IN THE WASH (2009)   171

A BIZARRE BABY BUMP (2009)   173

CHINA'S INVENTIVE VIGILANTE (2009)   175

A POSTHUMOUS PROJECTILE (2009)   177

BATTERIES NOT INCLUDED (2010)   179

GOING UNDERGROUND (2010)   181

BROUGHT DOWN TO EARTH (2011)   183

SOZZLED IN THE SADDLE (2011)   185

MILLAR'S ILLEGAL MILESTONE (2011)   188

THE HEIGHT OF INGENUITY (2012)   190

THE BIG CHILL (2012)   192

PLAY YOUR CARD RIGHT (2012)   194

JUST MARRIED! (2012)   196

JAMIE'S ROAD TO NOWHERE (2012)   198

CARRY ON, DOCTOR (2012)   200

FROOME'S AFRICAN ADVENTURE (2013)   202

THE SKY'S THE LIMIT (2013)   204

THE NEED FOR SPEED (2013)   206

SHANGHAI HIGH RISE (2013)   208

THE BICYCLE BANDITS (2013)   210

IT'S NOT ALWAYS GOOD TO TALK (2013)   212

CANADIAN CARDBOARD CAPER (2013)   214

THE GREAT 'JP' MYSTERY (2013)   216

THE FASHION POLICE (2013)   219

THE GREAT FALL OF CHINA (2015)   221

HALF-INCHED IN AMSTERDAM (2015)   223

STRONG-ARM TACTICS (2015)   225

BICYCLING IN THE BUFF (2016)   227

FIGHT THE FIREPOWER (2016)   229

DANGER, DANGER, HIGH VOLTAGE! (2016)   231

TABLES TURNED ON DJ (2016)   233

NOTTINGHAM'S MYSTERY URBAN ARTIST (2016)   235

AN UNEXPECTED TURN IN THE TOUR (2016)   237

MARSUPIAL BREAST ENLARGEMENT (2016)   239

THE CAR PARK RODEO (2016)   241

BIBLIOGRAPHY   244

CYCLING HISTORY TIMELINE   246

Nothing compares to the simple pleasure of riding a bike.

John F. Kennedy

INTRODUCTION

'As a kid I had a dream,' John Lennon once said. 'I wanted to own my own bicycle. When I got the bike I must have been the happiest boy in Liverpool, maybe the world. I lived for that bike. Most kids left their bike in the back yard at night. Not me. I insisted on taking mine indoors and the first night I even kept it in my bed.'

The late, great Beatle was, of course, just one of a global army of cyclophiles. With an estimated billion or so bikes in the world today, cycling has never had it so good in terms of bums on seats and tyres on tarmac, and whether it is a lazy, recreational pedal or lung-busting cyclo-cross action, from the thrills of BMX to the drama of the Tour de France, cycling is both one of the world's most popular pastimes and fastest growing sports.

Cycling's Strangest Tales charts the weird and wonderful evolution of the bicycle, the eccentric and controversial characters who have helped pioneer and popularise cycling and the oddest examples of two-wheeled mayhem on the planet.

It was back in the early 19th century that the German inventor Baron Karl von Drais first unveiled his 'laufmaschine' ('running machine'), the widely acknowledged template for the modern bicycle, unwittingly sparking a global phenomenon that shows absolutely no sign of abating.

Drais' wooden-framed contraption with two in-line wheels had no pedals and failed to make its designer his fortune – but his invention certainly made an enduring impression on an unsuspecting world in ways he probably could never have envisaged in his wildest dreams.

The pages that follow will explore the full gamut of surreal cycling stories and prove there really are absolutely no limits to what people will attempt given access to a saddle (or two), handlebars and two good wheels.

Many of our strange tales focus on the world of endurance riding and extreme cycling; ever since Thomas Stevens first successfully pedalled his way around the globe in the late 19th century, cyclists have been going faster, further and higher. Italy's Vittorio Innocente even managed to pedal away at a depth of 213ft (65m) underwater, while honourable mention must also go to astronaut Alan Bean, the first man to hop into the saddle in space.

The bizarre tale of the Polish cyclist who spends his spare time pedalling up the world's tallest skyscrapers has to be read to be believed, while the story of a two-wheeled assault on the South Pole is a timely reminder that the human spirit of adventure is very much in rude health.

Professional cycling may be more glamorous (and profitable) than its amateur cousin, but that doesn't make it a less rich source of unexpected anecdotes. From the moment money was at stake, racers have gone to increasingly nefarious lengths to ensure they were the first over the finishing line.

The Tour de France, for example, has seen riders amputating their own toes, the poisoning of rivals, surreptitious train rides and rioting on the streets in its long and sometimes chequered history. Other professional events have stood unwitting witness to shameful acts of bribery and corruption, an unexplained consignment of Viagra and an inner tube brimming over with urine. You will also have to read on to discover when Chris Froome's career was almost cut short by an angry hippopotamus, how Sir Bradley Wiggins' carnivorous tendencies nearly ruined his cycling dreams and why Sir Chris Hoy really owes it all to Steven Spielberg.

The bicycles themselves, however, remain the real stars of the show, and *Cycling's Strangest Tales* is replete with stories of the most unusual models and modifications on Drais' original, groundbreaking vision. Whether it is the American bike bristling with 13 shotguns welded to the frame, the cycle that can actually soar into the sky or the two-wheeler designed by Damien Hirst that sold for an eye-watering £325,000, we've got them covered.

It is also true to say that cycling has always attracted more than its fair share of eccentrics. Those who compete in the annual World Mountain Bike Bog Snorkelling Championship in Wales are certainly not what you'd call conventional cyclists, while the suited and booted competitors at the Brompton World Championships every year are verging on the bonkers. Why anyone would devote themselves to the 'art' of pedalling backwards while playing the violin will forever remain a mystery, and the Scottish gentleman inadvertently caught in an overly amorous embrace with his bike in 2007 was, we can surely all agree, simply deranged.

Bicycles, of course, are designed to get their riders from A to B without the inconvenience of walking but they have frequently been pressed into alternative service, and at various times our two-wheeled friends have played their part in invading China and doing the laundry, jumping over elephants and catching criminals. You can even make ice cream on a bike.

Cycling's Strangest Tales follows the colourful 200-year history of the bicycle and its legion of devotees with a mixture of reverence and amusement, proving that the writer H.G. Wells definitely had a point when he observed, 'Every time I see an adult on a bicycle, I no longer despair for the future of the human race.'

THE FALSE PRETENDERS
ITALY, 1478

To tell the story of the evolution of cycling, we must, of course, begin with the beautiful bikes themselves. Without them, this would be a disappointingly brief book and millions, perhaps billions, of people would have to find alternative forms of both transport and recreation.

There is, though, an initial problem in the recounting of the bicycle's fascinating history. We must first debunk the spurious but frequently repeated paternal claims of two inventions which have for too long tried to ride the bike bandwagon.

The first false claimant as the original bike focuses on a sketch allegedly penned by the one and only Leonardo da Vinci. It appears in his celebrated collected work *The Codex Atlanticus*, a huge compendium of his writing and drawings dating from 1478 to 1519, and to be fair, it definitely looks like a bike. Two wheels, pedals, a seat, the full monty.

The sketch was discovered in the 1970s, when the *Codex* was being restored by Italian monks, and what with Leonardo being widely regarded as a bit of a genius, everyone assumed it was safe to add 'inventor of the bicycle' to his already impressive CV.

But then the doubts surfaced, and by the 1990s most historians and experts accepted the suspiciously prophetic diagram was not exactly kosher.

'News of a bicycle-like sketch said to have been discovered during the ten-year restoring period of Leonardo da Vinci's *Codex Atlanticus* popped up in 1974, when literary historian Augusto Marinoni gave a lecture in Vinci, Leonardo's birthplace,' explained Prof. Dr Hans-Erhard Lessing at the eighth International Conference on Cycling History. 'From the chronology of disclosures and evidence, it is now becoming clear that we are dealing with a recent forgery.'

We don't know who 'added' the sketch of the bike, but it was not da Vinci. Unfortunately the *Codex* is now encased in plastic to preserve it for posterity, and the results of a carbon-dating test on the paper have never been made public.

The conspiracy theorists have had a field day, and the finger of blame has variously been jabbed at a pupil of Leonardo, a monk with a wry sense of humour who undertook the restoration work, and even Marinoni himself. The more prosaic truth is that we may never know.

The second imposter is a contraption dubbed the 'célérifère', allegedly invented by a chap called Comte Mede de Sivrac and apparently unveiled to an eager French public in 1790. A wooden-framed design boasting two wheels, a rudimentary seat but lacking handlebars to steer, it's a plausible if erroneous claimant but it was not until the 1970s that the célérifère was exposed as a false prophet.

The research revealed that de Sivrac was no more than an invention by French journalist Louis Baudry de Saunier in the late 19th century and the mythical célérifère no more than a patriotic hoax, an attempt to give a Frenchman the credit for giving the world the bicycle. Perhaps de Saunier can take comfort from the fact that even today there are plenty of Internet sites that continue to be taken in by his hoax.

FAME BUT NO FORTUNE FOR THE BARON
FRANCE, 1818

Now that we have exposed the twin charlatans that are da Vinci's drawing and the célérifère, the burning question remains: who the hell did invent the beloved bicycle? Who first came up with the beguilingly simple idea of mounting a couple of wheels on a frame and making a mockery of walking from A to B?

The truth is there was no single 'Eureka moment'. It's a story of evolution not revolution, of refinement and development rather than a fully formed birth, but most historians agree that the first authentic, totally legit forerunner of the modern bike was the 'laufmaschine', a machine invented by the ill-fated German, Baron Karl von Drais.

Also known as the 'velocipede', the wooden machine featured two wheels in tandem, a seat for the rider and a steering column. Pedals were yet to make an appearance in our story of the bicycle, and riders propelled themselves forward by pushing off from the ground with their legs.

After taking his invention for a couple of test rides, von Drais exhibited it to the public in Paris in 1818 and everyone was frightfully impressed. He was the toast of the French capital, and as the popularity of the velocipede steadily grew, he began to dream of the riches his ingenuity would bring.

He had, of course, overlooked one small thing. There were no patent laws to speak of in either France or his native

Germany back then, and once he had publicly shown his hand, there was precious little he could do to prevent anyone copying and modifying his original design. They say imitation is the sincerest form of flattery, but that's cobblers when you're trying to earn a living.

The latter years of von Drais' life were as turbulent as they were tragic. A political murder and his father's position as a leading provincial judge forced him to go into self-imposed exile in Brazil in 1822, and his fortunes did not improve significantly on his return to Germany five years later.

He headed to his hometown of Karlsruhe in the Baden region, but it was an area in the grip of simmering revolt and rebellion, and in 1849 fighting broke out between Republican rebels and the controlling Imperial forces of Prussia. Poor old von Drais publicly sided with the Republicans and when Prussia eventually emerged victorious from the regional squabble, they bankrupted him as punishment.

He died a penniless man just before Christmas in 1851, his laufmaschine never earning him either the recognition or the hard cash he deserved. Generations of cyclists however remain indebted to the unlucky German.

THE DANGERS
OF PEDAL POWER

SCOTLAND, 1839

The early bikes, inspired by Karl von Drais' design, were all well and good but they lacked a certain *je ne sais quoi*. Without pedals, they were akin to a potential masterpiece awaiting the final stroke from the artist's brush and, frankly, riders looked ridiculous pushing themselves along like frantic frogs.

The bike's prayers were finally answered in 1839 by an enterprising Scottish blacksmith by the name of Kirkpatrick MacMillan, and once he'd welded on a couple of well-placed pedals, cycling finally had lift-off.

The idea for pedals hit MacMillan when he began working as a blacksmith's assistant for the Duke of Buccleuch at Drumlanrig in Dumfriesshire. He noticed the inelegance of the people on their passing velocipedes and soon set his mind to finding a solution to the problem of propulsion and riders' incessant need to put their feet on the ground.

After a couple of dead ends, he had it. 'This first pedal bicycle was propelled by a horizontal reciprocating movement of the rider's feet on the pedals,' reads MacMillan's profile on the BBC website. 'This movement was transmitted to cranks on the rear wheel by connecting rods. The machine was extremely heavy and the physical effort required to ride it must have been considerable. Nevertheless, MacMillan quickly mastered the art of riding it on the rough country roads and was soon accustomed to making the 14-mile (22.5km) journey to Dumfries in less than an hour.'

Top work, fella, but even greater challenges lay ahead, and in June 1842 MacMillan embarked on a remarkable 70-mile (113km) journey from his home to Glasgow to put his new bike through its paces. It got him to the city, but the ride climaxed in the worst possible way when he knocked over a young girl in the Gorbals.

A Glasgow newspaper reported the following day how a 'gentleman from Dumfries-shire who bestrode a velocipede of ingenious design' had hit the girl and was fined five shillings. Thankfully she escaped with minor bruises, but cycling had just witnessed its first reported crash.

It would be remiss at this point not to concede that some historians are sceptical of the whole MacMillan story, but the weight of scholarly opinion remains behind our inventive Scottish blacksmith and his penchant for pedals.

For the record, the doubts relate to a chap named James Johnstone, who was MacMillan's nephew. Johnstone was anxious his uncle's achievement had been overlooked, and at the 1896 Stanley Show, he exhibited a replica of his bicycle in the hope of securing MacMillan's rightful place in the cycling annals.

The problem was the design he used actually belonged to a cartwright called Thomas McCall, who built two velocipedes of his own, complete with pedals, in 1869 and also manufactured the Stanley Show exhibit on behalf of Johnstone.

It's an interesting theory, but does beg the question why McCall would work for a man who was publicly trying to expunge him from the history books.

Like von Drais before him, MacMillan never enjoyed great financial rewards for his innovation, but that was because he never filed a single patent application or tried to sell his bike commercially, which is also why the sceptics suspect he may not be our man. They ignore, of course, the possibility that MacMillan simply was not cut out for a 19th-century equivalent of *Dragon's Den*.

HOW TO AVOID A WATERY
FALL AT THE WATERFALL

CANADA/USA, 1869

The Niagara Falls are like a magnet for madmen, sorry, intrepid daredevils who never seem to tire of devising dangerous and demented ways of crossing the cascade that separates Ontario in Canada and New York State in the USA.

It all started in the summer of 1859, when Frenchman Charles Blondin decided he was tired of life and determined to tiptoe across the gorge on a tightrope. Remarkably, he didn't die, and ever since then suicidal stuntmen and women have been throwing caution to the wind and traversing the Falls.

It was, of course, merely a matter of time before someone attempted to make the crossing on a bike on a tightrope, and the honour was to fall to a fella called Andrew Jenkins. Born in Gloucestershire, Jenkins emigrated to Canada in his childhood, and at the age of 15 his dad took him to see Blondin's spectacular stunt. Jenkins resolved he simply had to conquer Niagara himself. On two wheels.

His big day came in August 1869, and after securing a 4in (10cm) diameter rope across his chosen 1,050ft (320m) span, he readied himself for his leap of faith.

'A new candidate has made his appearance before the public for glory, renown and shekels,' reported *The Buffalo Express* the following day. 'He is called "Professor Jenkins" or "the Canadian Blondin" and his forte is riding the bicycle on a rope. Early in the day the crowd around the falls was far from small, and by noon the excursion trains on the Great Western and Lake Huron Railroads had brought thousands of people, all anxious to see the man ride over the falls on the velocipede.

'At 2.30 o'clock the Professor made his appearance at a small house on the Canada side with the pieces of his machine, and at once proceeded to put them together, a task of no small labour. All being in readiness, the bicycle was fastened by a rope to the bank.

'He wore white tights, black velvet knee breeches, shoulder straps and cross belts of the same material, and on his head was placed a crown-shaped hat and all were profusely bedecked with tinsel and beads. His feet were covered with buff moccasins.

'Three pistol shots were then fired from the Canadian side and it was a "Go". The machine moved slowly forward, the rope swaying gently from side to side until he had passed about 50 feet [15.2m], when another opportunity was given the artist, after which he crawled along at a snail's pace to the middle of the abyss, where he raised and waved his hat and received a faint cheer in response.

'From the center to the American shore it was evidently hard work to propel the bicycle, but at last the edge of the cliff was reached, and then the welcome did ring with the applause of the people. The time occupied in passing over the rope was just 11 minutes.'

The 'Canadian Blondin' was pushing it, considering his English heritage, but he had made it across unscathed and fulfilled his childhood dream. Jenkins traversed the Niagara Falls just that one time, but cashed in on his new-found fame for the next 15 years, performing a similar high-wire act across, among other places, the Rocky River in Ohio.

Jenkins' challenge may sound surreal, but his effort was positively sane compared to the exploits of Maria Spelterini seven years later, when the Italian tightroped across the Falls firstly with her feet strapped into fruit boxes and then blindfolded. Miraculously, she made it safely over on both occasions.

CHANNELLING THE POWER

UK/FRANCE, 1883

The very essence of cycling is pedal power, but if you've ever piloted a pedalo, you'll be aware that you can also make waves on the water. Pedalling can get you from A to B on dry land, but with the right rigging and a life jacket you can also sail the Seven Seas with a spot of good old-fashioned legwork.

This duality was not lost on one William Terry back in 1883 when he made one of the earliest attempts to create a truly amphibious vehicle and cross the English Channel for a spot of duty-free shopping.

Young William began his journey on a tricycle in London and when he arrived in Dover, he hopped off, mounted the bike on top of a canoe and fixed paddle wheels to the rear axle. It wasn't quite as sophisticated as James Bond's white Lotus Esprit in *The Spy Who Loved Me*, but the contraption did work, and after 20 gruelling hours of pedalling Terry eventually made it to France.

Legend has it that he was collared on landing by *les gendarmes*, who were convinced he was a smuggler, and was only allowed to continue his onward journey to Paris after quite reasonably pointing out he'd have to be unbelievably brazen, not to say bonkers, to commit such a crime on a canoe-mounted tricycle.

Terry did, however, open the floodgates for similar cross-Channel tomfoolery, and in 1929 Aimee Pfanner made it from Continental Europe to dear old Blighty on what was known as a 'hydro-cycle', a regular bike frame mounted on two long floats and powered by paddle pedals.

It took our plucky French girl around 14 hours to complete her journey, contemporary newspaper reports solemnly telling their readership that 'during the trip she ate food, chiefly fruit'.

One of the fastest pedalled-powered jaunts from England to France came in 1962, when two chaps called Ronald Brooks and James Wood fixed a tandem onto floats. They surged their way across in just eight hours and 55 minutes, proving the old *Nineteen Eighty-Four* mantra 'Four legs good, two legs bad'.

THE AMAZING TRAVELS OF THOMAS

USA, 1884

The sense of adventure and pioneering spirit has been a hallmark of the British character for centuries, and ever since the likes of Sir Walter Raleigh and James Cook set sail in search of mythical lands and profitable new territory, Brits have been travelling the globe frequently armed with little more than a stiff upper lip, immaculately ironed shirts and a haughty disdain for the indigenous population.

In the world of cycling, Blighty has arguably never produced a more marvellous adventurer than Thomas Stevens, the first man to circumnavigate the globe on a bicycle. That's right, right around the whole ruddy world on two wheels.

Stevens' remarkable journey began in the United States in 1884. His original plan was to become the first to pedal across North America, and once he had acquired a 50in (127cm) Columbia 'Standard' penny-farthing for the challenge, he was good to go, and at eight o'clock on 22 April he set off from San Francisco.

According to the *Adventure Cyclist* magazine, our intrepid cyclist was as tanned as a nut and 'a man of medium height, wearing an oversized blue flannel shirt over blue overalls, which were tucked into a pair of leggings at the knee'. They added, 'A mustache protruded from his face.' He travelled light, packing his handlebar bag with only spare socks and a shirt, a raincoat which doubled as a tent, his bedroll and (just in case) a .38 Smith and Wesson revolver.

Following wagon trails, railways and the public roads, he made superb progress and on 4 August, he triumphantly pedalled into Boston to complete his unprecedented 3,700-mile (5,954km) trek.

'More than one-third of the route followed by Mr Stevens had to be walked,' reported *Harper's Weekly*. 'Eighty-three-and-a-half days of actual travel and 20 days stoppage for wet weather made 103½ days occupied in reaching Boston. He followed the old California trail most of the way across the plains and mountains, astonishing the Indians, and meeting with many strange adventures.'

He was not finished yet. After spending the winter in New York he took a boat to England and prepared to get back in the saddle once again, setting off from Liverpool on 4 May 1885.

'A small sea of hats is enthusiastically waved aloft and a ripple of applause escaped from 500 English throats as I mount my glistening bicycle,' Stevens reminisced in the account of his epic adventure, *Around the World on a Bicycle*. 'With the assistance of a few policemen, 25 Liverpool cyclers who have assembled to accompany me out extricate themselves from the crowd, mount, and fall into line two abreast and merrily we wheel down Edge-lane and out of Liverpool.'

He caught a ferry from Newhaven to Dieppe but Continental Europe posed him few problems and he pushed on to Persia, where he spent the winter in Tehran as the guest of the Shah. His reputation, it seemed, preceded him.

There were, of course, obstacles along the route. There was the near-constant threat of an unwelcome contretemps with bandits, he was refused permission to cycle through Serbia, he was kicked out of Afghanistan by the local authorities after a little misunderstanding and he had to be given refuge from rioters in China when he inadvertently stumbled into a spot of local bother.

He was, however, nothing if not persistent, and on 17 December 1886 he reached Yokohama in Japan. His days of pedalling were over, as he dryly noted in his book. 'Distance actually wheeled,' he wrote, 'about 13,500 miles [21,726km].'

Stevens' adventuring days were not quite over and after an invitation by the *New York World* newspaper in 1888, he set off on an expedition to find the AWOL explorer Stanley in East Africa. He also jaunted off to Russia and sailed the rivers of Europe before returning to Britain, getting married and enjoying the rather more sedate pace of life that came with his job as the manager of the Garrick Theatre in London.

There is yet one more footnote to this amazing story and that's the fate of Thomas' trusty penny-farthing. After finishing his marathon in the saddle in Japan, he sailed back to San Francisco in January 1887 and the bike was bought by the famous cycle manufacturer, The Pope Company.

They diligently preserved the record-breaking machine for over 50 years but committed cycling history sacrilege when the Second World War broke out, donating Stevens' indefatigable companion to a scrap-metal drive. Despite its questionable suspension and dubious ride comfort, the old Columbia 'Standard' deserved better.

CYCLING'S DEBT TO STARLEY

ENGLAND, 1885

We have just shared the amazing story of Thomas Stevens' jaunt across the globe on his faithful Columbia 'Standard' (see 'The Amazing Travels of Thomas', page 25) but the truth is the first generation of penny-farthings were an absolute bugger to ride.

Perched precariously 5ft (1.4m) in the air, the rider required the balance of a Bolshoi ballerina to avoid toppling over and the leg power of Sir Chris Hoy to get the unwieldy contraption moving, and was generally about as safe as Greek Government bonds.

In short, the cycling revolution desperately needed a more manageable machine.

'However enthusiastic one may have been about the ordinary [penny-farthing],' wrote the journalist W.F. Grew in 1921, 'there is no denying that it was only possible for comparatively young and athletic men, and if it had remained the only bicycle obtainable, the pastime and the utility of cycling would never have reached its present state of popularity.'

Step forward John Kemp Starley, the man widely credited with providing the much-needed template for the modern bicycle.

Born in London in 1854, Starley moved to Coventry at the age of 18 to work with his inventor uncle. Five years later he met local cycling enthusiast William Sutton, and the new chums decided to go into business, forming the somewhat prosaic Starley & Sutton Co.

The dynamic duo initially built tricycles, but with the mantra 'two wheels are better three' ringing in their ears, they turned their attention to how to solve a problem like a penny-farthing. They rebranded the company in 1883 as Rover, and two years later they were ready to change the history of cycling.

They unveiled their creation in 1885 at the Stanley Cycle Show in London, Britain's main annual bicycle exhibition. They called it the Rover Safety Bicycle and to say it was a hit with the public would be an understatement.

The big deal was, of course, the design. Featuring two nearly equal-sized wheels, there was a hell of lot less chance of falling off. It was a rear-wheel drive, a significant departure from the old penny-farthings. The front forks directly steered the bike. You didn't need to be an Olympic gymnast to pilot one.

'I felt the time had arrived for solving the problem of the cycle,' Starley explained in a lecture more than a decade after his invention was unveiled. 'I therefore turned my attention solely to the perfection and manufacture of the Rover bicycle.

'The main principles which guided me in making this machine were to place the rider at the proper distance from the ground, to place the seat in the right position in relation to the pedals, and to place the handles in such a position in relation to the seat that the rider could exert the greatest force upon the pedals with the least amount of fatigue.

'My aim was not only to make a safety bicycle, but to produce a machine which should be the true Evolution of the Cycle, and the fact that so little change has been made in the essential positions, which were established by me in 1885, proves that I was not wrong in the cardinal points to be embodied to this end.'

The new Rovers flew off the shelves and it was not long before manufacturers across the world were copying Starley's basic design. The 'modern' bicycle had been well and truly born.

The man himself died in 1901 aged just 46, but his legacy in the world of cycling remains unquestioned.

'His Rover Safety revolutionised not just the bicycle but the world,' said Phillip Darton, the executive director of The Bicycle Association of Great Britain, in a 2012 interview. 'The billions of bicycles made since 1885 can trace their ancestry back to that original ground-breaking machine.'

A fascinating if treacherous footnote to Starley's story is the fact the Rover company began manufacturing motorcycles and cars three years after his premature death, hardly a touching tribute to the man who founded the company and devoted so much of his life to pedal rather than petrol power.

THE TYRE WARS

NORTHERN IRELAND, 1887

The human spine is a remarkable bit of biological engineering, but, as many are painfully aware, it can be utter agony when something goes wrong with all those delicate, temperamental vertebrae. In a recent completely made-up survey on the nation's biggest annoyances, back pain came in ahead of the VAT man, adverts for webuyanycar.com and Spanish air-traffic controllers.

Spare a thought then for the poor folk who were forced into the saddle in the early days of cycling, when the luxuriously pneumatic tyre was but a distant dream and shattered spines were all too commonplace.

The forerunner of the inflatable tyre we know and love today was an unforgiving band of iron moulded around a wooden wheel, and while this did offer a degree of protection to the fragile inner wheel, no such courtesy was extended to the equally fragile derrière of the rider who greeted the sight of a cobbled street with the same enthusiasm a condemned prisoner welcomes the firing squad.

In 1887, however, cycling learned the name of its saviour. The new messiah was Scotsman John Boyd Dunlop, who, after spending ten years working as a vet, turned his considerable intellect to the thorny issue of his son's maddeningly uncomfortable tricycle and, hey presto, he invented the inflatable tyre. It probably wasn't quite that straightforward, but you get the picture.

Dunlop applied for a patent in 1888 and when Irish cyclist Willie Hume became the first rider to win a few races on a bike with the new-fangled pneumatic tyres at a meeting in Belfast, the world sat up and took notice.

Except Dunlop didn't invent the pneumatic tyre. To be fair, he thought he was the first man to champion the comfort of cyclists' backsides, but at this stage of the story we must introduce Robert William Thomson, a fellow Scot who actually beat Dunlop to the punch by some 42 years.

Thomson hit on the idea of an inflated inner tube protected by a durable rubber 'outer' in the 1840s. He was granted a patent in France in 1846 and in the USA in 1847, and later that year exhibited his 'Aerial Wheels' in action on a horse-drawn carriage in Regents' Park in London. When his new invention failed to make his fortune, Thomson contented himself with working for a sugar-cane company in Java, as well as trying to perfect a self-filling fountain pen, before returning to Scotland and dying in 1873. When the assignees of his patent heard of Dunlop's development they protested to the relevant authorities, and the 'second' patent was withdrawn in 1890.

Dunlop sold his now seemingly worthless patent to an English entrepreneur called Harvey du Cros in 1896 for what proved to be a modest £3,000. Du Cros formed the Dunlop Pneumatic Tyre Company and he went on to earn a considerable packet from the Dunlop rubber brand.

Dunlop, meanwhile, died in Dublin in 1921. He was far from a pauper when he passed away but, like Thomson, must have felt a little, ahem, deflated that his idea never made much of an impact on his bank balance.

THE WRIGHT STUFF

USA, 1892

The names of Orville and Wilbur Wright are indelibly associated with the invention of the aeroplane and the maiden flight of their famous 'Wright Flyer' back in 1903. It's a cracking claim to fame but it's often scandalously overlooked that the boys cut their mechanical teeth repairing and designing bicycles. In fact, the bicycle also played an important role in the first plane engine.

It was in 1892 that the brothers founded The Wright Cycle Company in Dayton, Ohio. Like any good businessmen, they quickly expanded into renting and selling bikes as well as fixing them, and it wasn't long before they began designing them too.

Their 'Van Cleve' and 'St. Claire' models were unveiled in 1896. They were successful enough, but it was the priceless experience the Wrights gleaned from the engineering process that was to prove crucial to their later work.

Oh and the money, which they took out of the company and invested in a homemade wind tunnel where they could indulge their growing fascination with air travel. The boys were getting closer to their date with destiny.

There remained, however, one big problem. They had designed and built the Flyer's frame, they were happy enough with the angle of the wings and they'd found a dashing pair of goggles to wear. Their big headache was the engine and, unable to source a suitable car engine for the job, they commissioned Wright Cycle Company employee Charlie Taylor to build a customised solution.

Taylor dutifully cracked open his toolbox and created an engine that powered the Flyer's twin propellers by a sprocket chain drive. Sound familiar? Of course it does, it was basically a bigger and sturdier version of a bicycle chain. The Wright boys liked what they saw, fitted the engine and prepared for liftoff.

The rest is aeronautical history, but sadly from a two-wheeled perspective, the brothers' soaring success inevitably turned their heads and they lost interest in the Wright Cycle Company. It closed down in 1909, but it's certainly worth reminding the modern Boeing Dreamliner or Airbus A380 of the debt they owe to the humble bicycle and its chain.

ANSWERING THE CALL OF NATURE

FRANCE, 1893

Professional cycling isn't all about speed, power and fitness. Riders, of course, have to be fine physical specimens with thighs the size of tree trunks, but racing is also a battle of wits and planning. Tactics can make all the difference between the euphoria of success and the misery of failure, and those who innovate frequently prevail.

A leading early exponent of thinking outside the box was Charles Terront, arguably the first superstar of French cycling and a man who, as we shall see, was acutely aware that the mind is the body's most powerful muscle.

Terront's quick thinking was certainly in evidence in 1893, when he was invited to race against compatriot Valentin Corre in a 1,000km (621-mile) challenge staged at the Galerie des Machines in Paris. The two rivals were to go *mano a mano* – the first rider over the line takes all.

The race was certainly a marathon rather than a sprint, but the two protagonists were evenly matched, and as the hours slowly passed, there was little to choose between them. What could possibly separate the two gladiators of the saddle?

The pivotal moment came after 27 hours of pedalling when Corre finally accepted the inevitable, dismounted and hurried off for a long overdue 'comfort break'. Terront, however, ploughed on, and by the time Corre returned to the track, he found himself 2.5km (1½ miles) adrift.

Corre no doubt reasoned that he would make up the ground he had lost when Terront was forced to stop and pay his own visit *à la toilette*, but the moment never materialised, and three hours later it was Corre who once again was forced to pull over and dash to the urinals, losing yet more precious time. Answering the call of nature ultimately cost him the race as Terront completed the 1,000km in a time of 41 hours and 50 minutes, a comfortable 9.3km (5¾ miles) clear of his rival.

It was only when Corre's back-up team picked up the morning newspapers that they discovered Terront's secret courtesy of an eagle-eyed journalist, who revealed the winner did not in fact boast a bladder the size of a small swimming pool.

Terront had cut one of his inner tubes in half and tied a knot at one end. Whenever he felt the unmistakeable need to lighten the load, he would call over one of his support riders who would pull up alongside him and hand him the tube. Discreetly lowering it into his shorts, Terront would let nature takes its course and then merrily continue pedalling towards victory.

Corre had been comprehensively outwitted. 'Terront didn't even beat me by a tyre,' he wryly told journalists after the race. 'He won by an inner tube.'

Terront won 54 major events during his 15-year career. He was twice crowned the French champion and also triumphed in the British national championship, but in terms of sheer audacity, he never quite surpassed the cunning ruse he'd deployed in Paris.

FRANK'S FATAL FORAY

USA, 1894

It was but a few pages earlier that we learned of the remarkable global exploits of England's Thomas Stevens, the first man to traverse the planet on two wheels (see 'The Amazing Travels of Thomas', page 25). The redoubtable Thomas was nothing if not a pioneer, and ever since he completed his epic journey in 1886, other intrepid (some might say insane) cyclists have been inspired to follow in his iconic tyre tracks.

One of the very first was an American by the name of Frank Lenz. Frank had caught the cycling bug growing up in Pennsylvania, and in May 1892, cheered on by an enthusiastic crowd some 800 strong, he set off from Pittsburgh on his trusty Victory safety bicycle in a bold attempt to pedal himself around the world. National pride was at stake and, having struck a deal with *Outing* magazine for updates of his adventure, his American supporters waved him off furiously and awaited dispatches.

Frank headed to the West Coast and San Francisco, boarding a ship to Japan. He crossed China – which he reported was not to his liking due to the terrible state of the country's roads – and after many, many miles he reached Burma. The Burmese jungle proved as unhelpful as the aforementioned Chinese roads, but Frank ploughed on regardless, and didn't even let a little bout of malaria slow him down unduly. By late 1893 he was in India, followed by Persia, but it was during the summer of 1894, when he reached Turkey, that things went completely pear-shaped.

Frank was heading to the city of Erzurum in the east of the country. He never got there, and after a few months of radio silence, *Outing* and his family and friends became increasingly concerned, and another noted American cyclist called William Sachtleben was sent to investigate Frank's disappearance.

Sachtleben sailed to Europe in March 1895 and after having to forge papers to enable him to enter Kurdistan, he started asking questions. He did not like the answers he received one little bit. According to the locals, Frank had accidentally insulted an unsavoury Kurdish tribal leader on his travels, and the chief's followers had subsequently ambushed and then murdered him, burying the body by the banks of a river. Frank's epic journey had, it seemed, come to a rather grisly end.

The Turkish authorities charged the tribal leader with blood on his hands with murder and he was convicted, but it was a hollow victory as he had already fled the area. The USA, however, refused to let the matter drop, and after eight years of diplomatic pressure, the Turkish government finally agreed to pay Frank's mother $7,500 in compensation for his death.

It was of course no compensation at all. His body was never found, and one of cycling's great adventurers was sadly denied the proper burial he deserved.

ALL THAT GLITTERS
IS NOT GOLD

GREECE, 1896

The Olympics have produced some of British cycling's most magnificent and memorable moments in recent years, but the nation's two-wheeled love affair with the Games began back in Athens in 1896, with the first Olympics of the modern era.

A modest 19 cyclists from just five countries were in Greece to compete in the six separate events, five of which were staged at the Neo Phaliron Velodrome, while the road race was a 54-mile (86.9km) route from Athens to Marathon and back.

Britain sent a grand total of two riders, long-distance racer Edward Battel and endurance competitor Frederick Keeping, and both did us proud, with Eddie coming third on the road and Freddy second in the 12-hour time trial.

The strange thing about the 1896 Games, though, was the fact the winning riders of the six inaugural races received silver rather than gold medals. The French team, who provided four of the six champions, were absolutely spitting.

The lack of gold medals was not a result of an economy drive by the Olympic organisers, but rather a nod to the ancient Games, in which winners were presented with an olive branch and hard currency rather than a shiny bauble around their necks.

The Athens organisers broke with tradition in commissioning artist Nicolas Gysis to design a silver and bronze medal for the 1896 Games, for the winners and runners-up respectively, but no gold medal. The medals featured a portrait of Zeus on one face and a representation of the Acropolis and the Parthenon on the other.

Gold medals for Olympic winners made their first appearance at the 1904 Games in St Louis, which was jolly good news for the Americans, who won all seven on offer in the cycling. A seemingly impressive feat, until you realise that the States provided all 18 riders at the Games and no other country was represented.

Britain finally struck gold at the 1908 Olympics in London as Victor Johnson won over 660 yards (604m), Benjamin Jones triumphed in the 5,000m (5,468-yard) event, Clarence Kingsbury was the 20km (12½-mile) champion and Charles Bartlett was quickest over 100km (62 miles). And by the way, in 1908 11 nations competed in the cycling event, unlike the previous Olympics. The gold rush was completed with victory in the team pursuit and Team GB departed en masse to celebrate their sensational success.

THE HEART OF THE MATTER

ENGLAND, 1896

Aside from the potential discomfort of saddle sores and the inconvenience of an occasional stiff neck, the health benefits of cycling have been extensively documented over the years. Increased aerobic capacity, a strengthened immune system and a pair of impressively ripped calves are just some of the rewards for the frequent pedaller, and were it not for the perennial danger of HGVs on metropolitan roads or errant cows in Cumbria, cycling would probably be crowned the greatest form of exercise on the planet.

In the late 19th century, however, not everyone was so enamoured by the physical benefits of the bicycle. Some remained adamant that regular Morris dancing rather than cycling was a better form of exercise while others argued life in the saddle was actually a serious health risk.

Dr George Herschell was definitely in the latter camp. A senior physician at the National Hospital for Diseases of the Heart in London, by his own admission George was a regular cyclist himself but despite the shiny Raleigh in his shed, he was worried that too much pedalling could cause severe medical problems.

In 1896 he wrote an article in *The Lancet* headlined 'On Cycling as a cause of Heart Disease'. The clue was very much in the title as George expounded on his theory that bikes could be bad for you.

'Cycling, rationally pursued, is one of the most health-giving forms of amusement; but when indulged in to excess, or under improper conditions, one of the most pernicious,' he warned. 'Moreover it is of great interest to me, as I am myself a practical cyclist. I am sorry to say that during the last few years a considerable number of cases of heart disease, undoubtedly caused by cycling, have come under my observation.

'The chief danger of cycling, or rather the reason why it is more injurious than some other forms of exercise, is the probability when riding alone of being led into an injurious excess of exertion, and the almost certainty of the same thing happening when riding in company, especially with a club.'

Crikey, who knew? George did rather fail to empirically prove that heart disease was 'undoubtedly' the result of over-vigorous riding, but he wasn't finished yet and went on to warn parents of the terrible dangers of buying their child a bike for his or her seventh birthday.

'When we allow a child to ride long distances upon a cycle,' he wrote, 'we are carrying out a physiological experiment which, although possibly of interest from a scientific standpoint, must be utterly unjustifiable.'

George's thesis failed to gain much traction within the medical fraternity. His central argument that 'on no account should the cyclist continue riding after he has commenced to feel short of breath' was widely dismissed by his professional peers on the basis that it rather ruled out any form of exercise at all and he was talking cobblers.

The good doctor wrote many other pamphlets for *The Lancet* during his career. 'On Cycling as a cause of Heart Disease' was certainly one of the most contentious published, but he arguably surpassed it with his seminal 'The Treatment of Constipation by the injection of Olive Oil'.

THE LAST MADISON SQUARE MARATHON

USA, 1898

A week may be a long time in politics, but in America in the late 19th century, a mere six days must have felt like an absolute eternity for the riders who were brave or foolhardy enough to enter the Madison Square Garden 'six-day' event, a race so insanely gruelling that it should have come with a health warning, or at the very least some heavy sponsorship from a certain energy drink brand.

First staged in New York in 1891, the race, as the name suggests, was a straight endurance test staged over six consecutive days in which the competitors simply had to clock up as many miles as possible. Sleep was merely an optional extra and in theory the riders could pedal non-stop for the full six days. That's a potential 144 hours non-stop, or 8,640 minutes without a break.

The race initially proved hugely popular, but as the competitors pushed themselves harder and harder and suffered more and more, the sense of disquiet grew.

'It is a fine thing that a man astride two wheels can, in a six-day race, distance a hound, horse or a locomotive,' ran an editorial in *The New York Times* after the 1897 instalment of the race. 'It confirms the assumption, no longer much contested, that the human animal is superior to the other animals.

'But this undisputed thing is being said in too solemn and painful a way at Madison Square Garden. An athletic contest in which participants "go queer" in their heads, and strain their powers until their faces become hideous with the tortures that rack them, is not sport. It is brutality. Days and weeks of recuperation will be needed to put the Garden racers in condition, and it is likely that some of them will never recover from the strain.'

Things reached a head in 1898 when Charlie Miller was crowned champion. The American racked up a staggering 2,088 miles (3,360km) in the six days of racing and spent just 15 hours off the track, sleeping for only nine and a half. However, so many of the other competitors were hospitalised with exhaustion that the authorities decided enough was enough and ruled that riders could in future only spend a maximum of 12 continuous hours in the saddle before they were required to rest.

The new edict, however, did not bring an end to endurance cycling. The teams quickly realised that by entering two riders, with each racing for 12 hours each, they could easily circumvent the restrictions, and the modern Madison format – named in tribute to The Garden – was born.

And so 1898 was to be the last old-style race in New York but there is one fascinating footnote to the story, proving that while the physical demands of the event were far too much for some of the competitors, Miller at least was as fresh as a daisy.

It happened on the afternoon of the final day. Miller had established such a lead over his nearest rival that he could afford to abandon the track at 3.00p.m. An hour-and-a-half later he remerged to get married to a young lady by the name of Miss Hanson in front of the assembled spectators and after Miller had taken a victory lap of the track, the happy couple retired to the Waldorf-Astoria for their wedding night. It would, of course, be indelicate to speculate whether Mr and Mrs Miller had an early night or not.

NO PAIN, NO GAIN

FRANCE, 1904

It was Friedrich Nietzsche who said 'I assess the power of a will by how much resistance, pain, torture it endures and knows how to turn to its advantage.' The wily old German philosopher had clearly made the acquaintance of one or two professional racers.

Cycling has always been a tough gig. The agonising training is merely the *hors d'oeuvres* before the main event and in the melee of a frenetic race, accidents can and frequently do happen. Bikes get mangled and the riders often suffer much, much worse.

One of the most accident-prone but durable cyclists of the professional era has to be Bobby Walthour, one of the first superstars of the burgeoning American cycling scene in the late 19th century and early 20th century and a man who redefined what it meant to pedal through the pain barrier.

Born in 1878, Walthour began his career as a sprinter but initially found fame riding in the gruelling and controversial 'six-day' format in the States (see 'The Last Madison Square Marathon', page 43), winning in New York in 1901 and again two years later.

It was, though, in the world of 'motor-pacing' – the once hugely popular format in which cyclists would race in the slipstream of a motorbike to achieve the highest speeds possible – that Walthour really hit the heights, winning the American Championship twice before heading to Europe in

1904 and sweeping all before him. In total he won 11 of the 12 races in which he rode, and was so dominant the French media slightly erroneously dubbed him 'L'Imbattable Walthour', 'The Unbeatable Walthour'.

But motor-pacing was a dangerous endeavour and the litany of injuries Walthour suffered would surely have beaten a lesser man. During his career, he broke his left collarbone 18 times and his right 28 times. He accumulated a grand total of 115 stitches – 46 on his legs and 69 to his face and head – and he fractured his ribs 32 times. His eight broken fingers must have felt like little more than a minor inconvenience.

More seriously, he was twice pronounced dead at the scene after high-speed collisions with pace-setting motorbikes only to defy medical opinion, pick himself up and eventually return to the saddle.

Unbelievably Walthour was actually lucky in comparison to some of his motor-pacing contemporaries. Many died in the pursuit of even quicker times and it was undeniably a brutal way to go. Fellow America Harry Elkes was killed in front of 10,000 spectators in Boston when his rear tyre exploded at 60mph (96.6km/h) while George Leander did not live to regret his bold assertion that 'only the clumsy get themselves killed' when he was thrown 16½ft (5m) into the air during a race in Paris. He fell onto the track, bounced into the seating and died in hospital 36 hours later.

Walthour mercifully continued racing until the 1920s, but later life away from the track was not kind to him. 'His fortunes took a dramatic turn for the worse during the First World War,' wrote Andrew Holman in his Walthour biography *Life in the Slipstream*. 'Most of his considerable wealth, which had been deposited in European banks, was confiscated by the Germans after the war broke out. Walthour's personal life also began to unravel. His marriage ended in divorce after his wife, who had become infatuated both with alcohol and another man while Walthour was away in France during the war, tried to kill him with a butcher knife.'

Motor-pacing, in comparison, probably came as a very welcome distraction.

THE TOUR'S EARLY TROUBLES

FRANCE, 1904

Readers of a more mature vintage will remember the old British Rail slogan 'Let the train take the strain'. Sadly too few commuters heeded the company's pithy, poetic invitation and dear old BR was privatised, but the concept was essentially sound.

It proved a very bad idea, however, when Maurice Garin decided public transport rather than pedal power was the way forward during the 1904 Tour de France, an ill-advised move that saw the French rider stripped of the title and one of the most controversial Tours in history reach a dramatic and shameful denouement.

To describe the 1904 race, the second staging of the event, as mired in unseemly incident and general skulduggery would be an understatement. An understatement akin to dismissing Sir Chris Hoy's thighs as 'a bit big'.

From day one there was trouble. Garin and fellow French rider Lucien Pothier were ambushed and roughed up by four masked men, a competitor was disqualified for having 40 winks on the back seat of a car, another was caught slipstreaming behind another car, and at one stage organisers had to fire shots into the air to disperse an angry crowd who had attacked the peloton in a bid to help local boy Antoine Fauré establish a lead. The mob did eventually disband, but not before they'd knocked Italy's Giovanni Gerbi unconscious in the melee.

At other times, nails were spread over parts of the course, rocks thrown at the cyclists and barricades erected. It was complete and utter madness.

It's easy, then, to imagine the feelings of sheer relief the organisers, let alone the riders, must have initially felt when the anarchic tour finally came to an end in Paris on 23 July, but the drama was far from over.

No sooner had Garin popped the champagne and posed for the mandatory pictures with the pretty girls who are always in attendance at such events than the allegations of cheating began to pour in. Specifically, the winner was accused of taking the train during part of the race when he ought to have been in the saddle.

It may seem a preposterous allegation today. We live in a world of GPS, satellites and 24/7 live television coverage, but back then riders were merely given route maps and told to register in each major town they passed through along the way. There were far fewer prying eyes to confute the cheats.

The Tour organisers really didn't want the bad publicity of an investigation but the *Union Vélocipédique Française* (UVF) stepped in, interviewed dozens of witnesses and eventually handed Garin a two-year ban for letting the train take the strain. The second, third and fourth-placed riders were also stripped of their finishes, and fifth-placed Henri Cornet, a fresh-faced 19-year-old, was declared the winner.

For the record, Garin never admitted his guilt, and the UVF paperwork connected to the investigation was subsequently lost during the First World War when it was hastily sent south as the Germans invaded, never to resurface again. A grand total of 29 riders were found guilty of a series of offences and the nascent event was on its knees.

'The Tour de France is finished and I'm afraid its second edition has been the last,' sobbed its founder Henri Desgrange. 'We have reached the end of the Tour and we are disgusted, frustrated and discouraged.'

Desgrange was, of course, wrong, but it's impossible to stress how close the famous old race came to a premature and controversial end over a century ago.

THE TOUR'S MYSTERY MAN

FRANCE, 1904

Since the first staging of the Tour de France back in 1903, thousands of riders have girded their loins, saddled up and accepted the legendary challenge of cycling's grandest and most gruelling Grand Tour event.

Some have found fame and fortune thanks to the Tour, while others have struggled to make a significant impact. And then we have Georges Goffin, an elusive Belgian rider from the early 20th century who is arguably the worst competitor in the history of the Tour.

Details about Goffin's career are sketchy to the say the least. We do know he was born in Liège in French-speaking Belgium, he sometimes raced under the name of Georges Nemo, and he first entered the Tour in 1904. In total he rode in five Tours, but on each occasion he failed to even complete the first day's racing, a spectacular record of premature failure that no one else has ever come close to emulating. No one is quite sure exactly why the Belgian was unable to finish the first stage five separate times.

'The record of Belgium's Georges Goffin was one of persistent failure,' says *The Yellow Jersey Companion to the Tour de France*. 'Almost nothing is known about him, including why he rode under different names.'

Goffin, however, does not hold the record for the shortest ever Tour, a dubious distinction that goes to Englishman Chris Boardman after he lasted just 90 seconds in 1995.

In fact, Boardman didn't even ride in the Tour proper that year, crashing on a bend in Brittany during the prologue stage of the event, which resulted in an unscheduled trip to the local hospital.

'Storms flooded Brittany,' wrote French historian Jean-Paul Ollivier. 'The British rider came out of the start ramp like a rocket, took two or three bends at the very limit, a true acrobat, and went without limit through a wider bend. Propelled by his rare strength, his back wheel lifted into the air, hitting the barrier on the right of the road. [Team manager] Roger Legeay, who was following him by car, barely managed to miss him. Tally, several breaks to an ankle, cuts to his forearm, multiple bruises. Before it had even started, the Tour was finished without him.'

It took two hours of surgery to repair the damage to Boardman, which was exactly one hour, 58½ minutes longer than his race had lasted.

CHRISTOPHE BATTLES THE ELEMENTS

ITALY, 1910

The 'Milan-San Remo' race is one of the five fabled 'Monuments' of European cycling, an acknowledged classic on the Continental racing calendar. At 298km (185 miles) long, it is also the longest one-day course on offer to professional riders, and attracts hundreds of entrants and thousands of spectators in April every year.

First staged back in 1907, the race was originally organised by *La Gazzetta dello Sport* as a publicity stunt, but it nearly came to a premature end in 1910 when unseasonably arctic conditions decimated the field and very nearly killed the eventual winner. The race's Italian nickname of *La Primavera* ('The Spring') presumably caught on much later.

Sixty-five intrepid competitors lined up for the start of the race on the freezing morning of 3 April. The average temperature for Milan at that time of year should have been a comfortable 57.2°F (14°C), but there was already snow on the ground and a bitter wind in the air.

Our brave winner was a Frenchman by the name of Eugenio Christophe, who finished the course in a time of 12½ hours, but it's no exaggeration to say he could have died on the way as he battled the elements. 'Not far from the summit I had to get off my bike because I started feeling bad,' Christophe recalled years later: 'My fingers were rigid, my feet numb, my legs stiff and 'I was shaking continuously. It was bleak and the wind made a low moaning noise.

'In places there were 20cm [8in] of snow. Each time I was obliged to get off and push. Then I had to stop with stomach cramp. I collapsed on to a rock at the side the road. I was freezing.

'I saw a house not far away but I couldn't get there. I didn't realise just what danger I was in. Happily in my misfortune a man chanced to pass by. I nodded towards the house and said "casa" [house] and he understood. He took me by the arm and led me to the house, which was a tiny inn.

'The landlord undressed me and wrapped me in a blanket. I murmured "aqua caldo" [hot water] and pointed at the bottles of rum. I did some physical exercises and I started to get some feeling back in my body.'

Unbelievably, Christophe got back in the saddle to complete the race and collect the winner's cheque for 300 francs but it took him a full month in hospital to recover from the frostbite he suffered and another two years before he regained full fitness.

The rest of the field did not fare any better. According to some reports only three other competitors made it to the finishing line but other accounts state that fourth-placed Cyrille Van Hauwaert was disqualified for hanging onto the back of a car. If true, the Belgian should have been disqualified simply for not having the sense to get inside the motor.

DUBOC'S
WATER-BOTTLE WOE
FRANCE, 1911

Doping plagued the Tour de France for decades but it was the administration of different dubious substances that scandalised the 1911 instalment of the race, when Paul Duboc was the victim of a Machiavellian poisoning which would have left even Sherlock Holmes bewildered and bemused.

The background to the Frenchman's unwilling intoxication goes something like this. Riding for the La Française-Diamant team, Duboc was beginning to make inroads into the advantage established by Tour leader Gustave Garrigou after winning stages eight and nine in the Pyrenees, and the race was alive with talk of Duboc pinching the lead from his compatriot.

The 203-mile (327km), 10th stage between Luchon and Bayonne was the ideal opportunity for him to maintain his momentum, and after two hours' hard riding, Duboc had left Garrigou in his wake and pressed on.

It was now time for the aforementioned poisoning incident. Duboc passed a watering station and grabbed a bottle. He pedalled on for a few more minutes, but after quenching his thirst, he suddenly doubled up in pain and was unable to continue. Some unscrupulous person had nobbled his drink.

The race director Henri Desgrange later recalled rounding a bend in the road to see Duboc on the grass verge 'in a terrible state, struck with nausea that had turned him green, and suffering from terrible diarrhoea and painful vomiting. I smelled a bidon [water bottle] at his side and it didn't appear to me to have the odour of tea.'

Speculation about the identity of the poisoner was rife. Duboc's supporters pointed the finger at the Garrigou camp, while others blamed a mysterious disgruntled Tour rider with an axe to grind. *Les gendarmes* couldn't pin the Mickey Finn on anyone and the crime ultimately went unpunished.

To his credit, Duboc recovered sufficiently to pedal home 20 places behind Garrigou on the 10th stage and went on to win two more stages of the 1911 Tour. He eventually finished the race as runner-up to Garrigou, but we'll never know whether he could have been crowned champion had it not been for his enforced and rather gruesome-sounding break.

Duboc earned another dubious claim to fame during the 1919 Tour, when he broke a pedal axle. Desperate to repair the damage, he foolishly borrowed a car to find spare parts and was promptly disqualified by the race committee for cheating. Duboc protested his innocence but the organisers weren't budging.

DANGER IN THE DARKNESS

SWEDEN, 1912

When it comes to the definition of risky business, cycling in the dark in the middle of the night is right up there with crocodile wrestling, confessing to a fondness for Karl Marx at the Conservative Party annual conference or stubbornly clinging on to shares in Woolworths, Blockbuster or Friends Reunited.

Sadly the perils of nocturnal pedalling were ignored by the organisers of the 1912 Olympics in Stockholm when they sat down to finalise the plans for the road race at the Games. Their choice of course was fair enough – a scenic loop around the lovely Lake Mälaren just outside the capital – and while the scheduled route was an undeniably gruelling 198 miles (319km), everything seemed to be in order. They rather dropped a clanger, however, when they decided that the 123 competitors from 16 different nations would begin the big race at 2a.m.

It was asking for trouble, and that was certainly what happened as three riders suffered serious crashes in the gloom. In the aftermath of the race the Swedish Olympic Committee tried to gloss over the self-inflicted problems, but there was no disguising the chaos that had taken place.

'It was hardly possible to foretell what would happen at the grand road race. It could be seen, of course, from the entries, that the match would be an exceedingly keen one … There was an enormous crowd gathered at the starting place, and it [was] with the greatest difficulty that the local police and the soldiers who had been sent to their assistance could manage to keep just enough of the road clear for the passage of the competitors,' read the official race report.

'Besides one or two tumbles of the ordinary kind, and which were not at all dangerous, there were not more than a couple of accidents during the whole of this great competition, both of them, however, being, fortunately enough, of such a character that no lasting injury was caused to the sufferers.

'Stokes (England) broke his collar-bone at Södertälje and he was at once taken in hand by the doctor acting on behalf of the control committee there. The injured man was taken to the hospital where he received every attention, and was soon able to be removed to Stockholm by his fellow-countrymen.

'The other accident was a more serious one, and happened to one of the Swedish representatives, Mr Landsberg of Örebro, only a few hundred metres from the start. He was trying to get out of the way of a motor-waggon, but he was run into, his cycle smashed and he himself dragged along some distance before the waggon stopped. He was carried back to the starting place, whence he was conveyed to St Mary's Hospital, where he had to remain for some days.'

What the report failed to mention was the unfortunate Russian rider who crashed into a ditch and lost consciousness. He was subsequently found by a local farmer and rushed to hospital, his pride no doubt as dented as both his body and bike.

For the record, South Africa's Carl Schutte managed to stay on the course long enough to win the road race ahead of Brit Frederick Grubb and claim gold. He attributed his success to a diet of copious carrots and blind luck.

THE PELISSIER PROTEST
FRANCE, 1924

When we reluctantly turn our thoughts to the unedifying part doping has played in the history of the Tour de France and other events within professional cycling, we inevitably think of subterfuge, clandestine rendezvous with suppliers and, well, riders rather eager not to be exposed as cheats.

The 1924 Tour was startlingly different thanks to the Pelissier brothers – 1923 winner Henri and Francis – and what they revealed about what really went on behind the scenes during the famous race was as damning as it was ultimately unheeded.

The controversy was sparked by a heated row between Henri and race founder and organiser Henri Desgrange. A volatile and vocal man at the best of times, Henri Pelissier was incandescent with rage after Desgrange would not allow him to remove one of his racing jerseys as the heat of the day took effect. It was a rule, albeit petty, that riders had to finish a stage with exactly the same clothing they began it in, and Desgrange was not about to make any exceptions.

Henri had had enough. He quit the Tour, persuaded his brother Francis and fellow rider Maurice Ville to join his protest and then invited journalists to join them in the nearest café so he could vent at the iniquities of the Tour.

He initially limited his diatribe to lambasting Desgrange's rules and regulations but the talk then shifted to the excessive physical demands placed on the racers and how the riders coped with the miles and miles of racing.

'Do you want to see how we keep going?' Henri asked, reaching into a bag and producing a phial. 'That, that's cocaine for our eyes and chloroform for our gums.'

Ville tipped out the contents of his own bag to reveal boxes of mysterious pills. 'In short,' added Francis, 'we run on dynamite.'

The hacks hurried off to implore their editors to hold the front page but, in truth, the French public seemed more taken aback by the news of the withdrawal of their defending champion than his shocking revelations and amazingly Henri was allowed to ride the Tour again the following year.

He gave up cycling in 1927, but there was to be one more dramatic twist in what was a tumultuous life story. Henri's first wife Leonie committed suicide in 1933, shooting herself, and soon afterwards he began a relationship with Camille Tharault, who was 20 years younger than him.

It was to prove a stormy liaison, and in May 1935 it ended in further tragedy. After a bitter argument, Henri lunged at Camille with a knife at their villa outside Paris and cut her face. She fled to a bedroom where she found the same gun with which Leoni had killed herself two years earlier and confronted her lover. Henri lunged at her with the knife a second time and, whether in genuine self-defence or rage, Camille shot him five times.

'The tragic end of Henri Pelissier surprises no one,' reported the *Paris-Soir* newspaper. '"If I'd had the money I would have left him long ago," the murderess said yesterday.'

VICTOR DENIED VICTORY

1929

The relationship between a rider and his bicycle is essentially a simple one. The former provides the power and the latter bears the weight, and a cyclist really shouldn't be in the business of carrying his own bike around.

In the famous Tour de France of 1929, however, that's exactly what happened to Victor Fontan, a heartbreaking example of terrible luck, mechanical malfunction and eventual failure that led to a major overhaul in the rules of the race.

It all happened on the 10th stage of the Tour, a mountainous and gruelling 201-mile (323km) stretch from Luchon to Perpignan. It was such a long route that the riders had set out before dawn to ensure they would finish the stage and, as the race leader, Fontan proudly led them out wearing the yellow jersey.

He got less than 5 miles (8km) before disaster struck. According to some reports he crashed into a gutter while others insist he collided with a dog, but the end result was the same, his front forks were shattered and he needed another bike. The problem was that riders were not simply allowed to jump onto new wheels. They had to prove to the race judges that their bicycles were irreparably damaged ,and with the sun yet to rise on the 10th stage, there were no judges to be seen. Fontan had no second bike, no back-up team and, seemingly, no hope.

'Fontan was reduced to knocking on the doors of the villagers in the dark of the early morning looking for another bike that he might borrow,' relates Carol and Bill McGann in their book *The Story of the Tour de France*. 'At last he found a bike to resume the race, but he didn't just ride off. He couldn't. He had his broken bike strapped to his back. That year a rider had to finish with the bike he used to start the stage.'

For nearly 100 miles (161km), the Frenchman heroically pedalled on up and down the Pyrenees trying to catch the leaders with his mangled cycle weighing him down, but it was mission impossible and he was eventually forced to quit.

He came to a halt in the village of Saint-Gaudens and began to cry as he realised his chance of Tour glory had disappeared. It was the first Tour to be covered by radio and Fontan's sobbing was recorded by two reporters and broadcast later the same day, sparking a national debate about the rule that had cost him so dearly.

'How can a man lose the Tour de France because of an accident to his bike? I can't understand it,' wrote the journalist Louis Delblat in *Les Echoes des Sports*. 'The rule should be changed so that a rider with no chance of winning can give his bike to his leader, or there should be a car with several spare bicycles. You lose the Tour de France when you find someone better than you are. You don't lose it through a stupid accident to your machine.'

The public mood was sympathetic, and the following year the Tour organiser Henri Desgrange bowed to the pressure and legalised the use of replacement bikes as well as back-up teams, who could now help the riders with repairs. Fontan was back to compete again in the 1930 Tour as captain of the French team, but his big chance had been the previous year and there was no fairytale return.

THE BIG BINDA BRIBE

ITALY, 1930

Everyone loves a champion. The thrill of witnessing a leading sportsman or woman at the very top of their game is a transcendent treat and those able to take their chosen game to a new level are artists indeed. Sport, after all, is about creating heroes.

The Italian rider Alfredo Binda should have been one of racing's undisputed heroes during his career in the 1920s and 1930s but while he was imperious out on the road, he eventually proved something of a turn-off with the cycling authorities. His talent was unquestionable but his popularity was not.

The problem was Binda was just too bloody good. 'Il Campionissimo' ('The Champion') won the Giro d'Italia for the first time in 1925 and returned in 1927 to dominate the race once again, winning 12 of the 15 stages en route to the title. He was champion again in 1928 and made it a hat-trick of triumphs a year later.

No one could touch him and in recording three successive wins in the Giro, Binda won 33 of the total of 41 stages held. 'Cycling has always thrived off rivalry but Alfredo Binda never really had a proper rival,' explained John Foot in his book *Pedalare! Pedalare!* 'For much of his career he dominated the sport like a dictator (one of his nicknames) and his victories became so frequent that they almost became boring. A cult of personality developed around him, almost as if he were a god. He simply pulverised the opposition.'

The organisers of the Giro were getting fed up. The predictability of Binda's victories was beginning to impact on spectator numbers and *La Gazzetta dello Sport* newspaper wasn't shifting extra copies reporting yet another achievement by Alfredo.

Something had to be done, and after a clandestine meeting between Giro boss Emilio Colombo, Legnano team owner Emilio Bozzi and other assorted men in suits, it was decided to offer the unbeatable Binda a cash incentive – aka a large bribe – not to ride in the 1930 race.

Binda reportedly agreed it might well be time to let someone else have a crack at the title and agreed to sit this one out. There was one condition and that was his pay-off had to equate to the same as he would have earned had he won the Giro once again, plus additional cash for his projected six stage wins, his Legnano team bonus plus other bits and bobs. The final bill, he insisted, would be a whopping 22,500 lire. A smooth operator, our Alfredo.

Colombo and co were stunned. They'd budgeted for far less, but they'd come this far and reluctantly agreed to his demands, and the way was rather expensively paved for fellow Italian Luigi Marchisio to have his 15 minutes of fame.

Binda spent the summer of 1930 riding in the Tour de France. He won the eighth and nine stages of the race before pulling out, doubtless eager to leave enough time to spend his unexpected windfall on the French Riviera. He was, though, back on the winner's podium when he wrapped up a fifth Giro d'Italia title in 1933, as Colombo conceded he could no longer afford to keep Alfredo away.

OLYMPIC SKULDUGGERY
GERMANY, 1936

The men's 100km (62-mile) individual road race at the 1936 Olympic Games in Berlin was an absolute belter. A little less Nazi regalia draped around the Olympiastadion for the climax of the event would have been nice, but the cycling itself was superb.

The race came down to a shootout between fellow Frenchmen Guy Lapébie and Robert Charpentier. Lapébie hit the front inside the stadium with 100m (328ft) to go but was dramatically overhauled by his compatriot just before the line. Charpentier claimed gold and Lapébie, just 0.2 agonising seconds behind his teammate, had to settle for silver.

That would have been the end of that, but the action had been captured by director Leni Riefenstahl, a Nazi propaganda filmmaker who was a big fan of Adolf Hitler. Despite her dubious political views, she was jolly handy with a camera. The result of Riefenstahl's efforts was the film *Olympia* and when it was released in France, Lapébie headed to his local cinema for a look. He nearly choked on his popcorn when he saw the final edit.

Riefenstahl had done a superb job in filming the final moments of the road race. Lapébie watched himself enter the Olympiastadion. He saw himself hit the front of the pack. He witnessed Charpentier counterattack and then, to his horror, he saw his rival tug at the back of his shorts moments before going past him to take gold.

Quelle horreur! Lapébie was incandescent and wasn't slow to let everyone know he now believed he had been the victim of skulduggery. 'I was tugged backwards at the last moment,' he raged. 'From the day I saw that film, I considered myself the moral victor of the Olympic Games.'

Strong stuff, but Charpentier was in no mood to hold his hand up and swap medals. 'That is the biggest lie I have ever heard,' he responded. 'I'll sue Lapébie for defamation, even if it costs me a month's wages.'

Thanks to the wonder of modern technology and a well-known website that is replete with videos of kittens falling off washing machines, it's possible to see highlights of the contentious 1936 race but, sadly, it's inconclusive whether Charpentier was a massive cheat or Lapébie merely a bad loser.

The record books remain in the Charpentier camp, while Lapébie did at least win gold in the team road race and team pursuit in 1936. And one of his teammates in both those Olympic triumphs? Monsieur Robert Charpentier, of course.

WAR ON WHEELS

CHINA, 1937

When it comes to a spot of trouble in a war zone, tanks are traditionally the go-to vehicle. Your average Panzer or Sherman is simply brimming with heavy armour, machine guns and cannons and relishes the prospect of venturing where angels fear to tread and having a dust-up. Bicycles ... not so much, but that has not precluded our two-wheeled friends from playing a major role in a series of historical conflicts.

The first recorded use of bikes in battle was in South Africa in 1896, during a minor skirmish known as the Jameson Raid before the Second Boer War, but it was the ominous advent of World War One that saw cycles pressed into active service for the first time on a large scale.

All the main protagonists deployed cycle-mounted infantry as well as scouts, messengers and even medical personnel on bikes, but it was still the heavy artillery and (later in the war) tanks that held sway, and the intrepid souls who pedalled into action were very much the supporting cast.

The first major role for bellicose bikes came during the Second Sino-Japanese War in 1937, when 50,000 Japanese troops swarmed into China en masse in the saddle. Like the Spanish Inquisition, the Chinese definitely weren't expecting that, and the tactic proved hugely successful. So much so that the Japanese repeated the trick during the Second World War in the Malay Peninsula en route to capturing Singapore, using the speed of their free-wheeling soldiers through the jungle to outflank the retreating Allied Forces and generally cause mayhem.

During the Second World War the British employed airborne 'Cycle Commandos' who were issued with folding bikes, ordered to jump out of a plane and pedal off and bash the Bosch. The tactic was discontinued when the troops quite reasonably pointed out the sight of them unpacking their cycles tended to elicit giggles rather than fear from the German ranks.

In more recent years, the Viet Cong made good use of bicycles along the Ho Chi Minh Trail during the Vietnam War to transport supplies and avoid American napalm, but the advent of laser-guided missiles, drone planes and even bigger, badder bombs has sadly seen the bike's effectiveness in battle wane.

The last country to boast a full-time regiment of bicycle-mounted troops was Switzerland, but even they finally realised the folly of putting their national security in the hands of soldiers armed only with two wheels, puncture-repair kits and impossibly complicated penknives.

'The Swiss have decided that pedal power has no place in plans to modernise and professionalise the army,' reported the BBC in 2001 when news broke that the military cyclists were for the chop.

'During the Second World War, the cyclists defended Switzerland's borders against the threat of Nazi attack.

'Only the fittest of the fit get into the cycling regiment. Recruits face a rigorous training regime, which includes a 200km (124 mile) forced pedal march starting at two in the morning. The bikes weigh 25kg (55lb) without luggage and at least twice that fully laden with equipment including anti-tank weapons.

'But the government has decided that this unique brand of military service is no longer needed. In a new technologically advanced army, there is no room for the unprotected pedal pushers.'

A YEAR IN THE SADDLE

ENGLAND, 1939

Anglo-Australian sporting rivalry is a deadly serious business. The ongoing battle for supremacy between the old colonial power and the uncouth Antipodean upstarts, sorry, our proud Australian cousins, has defined both nations over the decades, and the intensity of battle shows no signs of abating.

It was the same story in cycling in the 1930s, with the two countries pedalling furiously for superiority in the saddle, and one of the most hotly contested disciplines was the gruelling world of endurance riding, a format in which riders would attempt to clock up the most miles in a single calendar year. It was, frankly, insanity on two wheels.

The two main protagonists in this tale of self-inflicted torture and torment were Australia's Ossie Nicholson and England's Tommy Godwin, and the tussle for national pride reached a head in 1937, when Nicholson set a phenomenal new record of 62,657 miles (100,834km) after 365 days on the road.

The Australian smugness was unbearable, and on 1 January 1939 Godwin set off at five o'clock in the morning in a bid to wrest the record back for dear old Blighty. It was the start of a remarkable journey that saw him crisscross the country as he relentlessly piled on the miles.

Godwin (not to be confused with the Olympic cyclist Tommy Godwin, who won bronze medals at the 1948

London Olympics) had bases in Stoke-on-Trent and Hemel Hempstead, and he planned his daily routes to end at either one so that he could conveniently collapse and, hopefully, recover in time for the next day's challenge. His bike was a four-speed, steel-framed mount supplied by his sponsors, Raleigh, and although it may have been state-of-the-art for the era, it was a distinctly unwieldy and heavy piece of equipment compared to its modern successors.

His 'fuel' for his epic trial was nothing more than a modest diet of bread, milk, eggs and cheese. Godwin had become a vegetarian after briefly working in a pie-making factory as a teenager and he was also teetotal, ensuring he was never hungover when he embarked on yet another energy-sapping early-morning start.

Nicholson's record was within sight and on 26 October, Godwin surpassed the Australian's accumulated mileage when he rode triumphantly into London.

'He prepared himself on this Thursday morning October 26, for a gentle ride to Trafalgar Square and the planned reception,' wrote Godfrey Barlow in his book *Unsurpassed: The Story of Tommy Godwin, The World's Greatest Distance Cyclist*. 'The ride turned out to be far from gentle as it was cold, wet and sleet was falling, making conditions far from ideal. The weather reminded Tommy of the day he set out back in January, 299 days ago.'

A proud nation rejoiced, Tommy was granted an audience with the Prince of Wales and it all went very quiet down under.

He was not finished yet though. After taking the day off for his impromptu royal engagement, Godwin was back in the saddle, and by the end of his day's riding on 31 December, he had clocked an incredible 75,065 miles (120,802km) in the year. That's a staggering average of 206 miles (332km) each and every day, the equivalent of cycling from London to Manchester. He spent an average of 18 hours each day riding and on 21 June recorded 361 miles (581km), his longest daily distance throughout the year.

No one would now have begrudged Tommy a thoroughly deserved rest but he was nothing if not determined, and despite having put Nicholson firmly in his place, he ploughed on. And on and on. His new target was to set a new record for the fastest man to clock up 100,000 miles (160,930km) and on 14 May, 500 days after setting off, he reached his milestone.

It was finally time for Tommy to get off the bike. He was so exhausted by his exertions that he reportedly complained of seeing pink elephants, and it took him weeks to be able to walk properly.

His feat was recorded in the fabled *Golden Book of Cycling* at the end of 1939 but his achievement no longer features in the *Guinness Book of Records* because the editors believe it would be total and utter madness for anyone to attempt to eclipse Tommy's record. They've probably got a point.

THE BRAVERY OF BARTALI

ITALY, 1943

We have already learned how bicycles have been deployed as instruments of aggression in times of conflict (see 'War On Wheels', page 67) but they have also been a force for good during combat, proving the humble cycle can actually save lives.

The two-wheeled hero of our story is Gino Bartali. The Italian famously won the Giro d'Italia twice as well as the 1938 Tour de France before the outbreak of the Second World War the following year, but whatever he achieved as a professional rider, he easily eclipsed with his fearless and selfless actions during the hostilities.

It was a terrible time for Italy's Jewish community. The formation of the Italian Social Republic in 1943, a puppet state controlled by Germany, saw the Jews persecuted and hunted by the Nazis and Italian fascists alike. Bartali did not like what he saw and decided to do something about it.

He made contact with the Italian and Jewish Resistance. Specifically, he began to courier forged travel documents to help Jews escape the country, riding out from his home in Florence every morning to collect photographs from those hiding in a local convent; with the pictures safely stashed in the frame of his bike, he'd return to the city and meet up with the forgers. The Italian police and the German troops were reluctant to search the celebrated cyclist, despite stopping him daily at their checkpoints, and under the pretence of training, Bartali was able to brazenly help thousands flee. According to a report by the Italian newspaper *Corriere della Sera* in 2003, some 800 Jews escaped as a direct result of his clandestine cycling.

He was eventually arrested by Mussolini's Blackshirts, taken to a villa infamous as a torture centre and ordered to stop his riding. 'I do what I feel,' he defiantly replied.

His heroics did not stop there, however, and when Nazi forces occupied Florence in 1943, he gave shelter to a displaced Jewish family in the cellar of his home in Via Del Bandino on the outskirts of the city, apparently dismissing the danger to himself and his own family had their guests been discovered by the Germans.

'The cellar was very small,' recalled Giorgio Goldenberg, one of the family saved by Bartali's bravery. 'A door gave way onto a courtyard, but I couldn't go out because that would run the risk of me being seen by the tenants of the nearby apartment buildings. The four of us slept on a double bed. My father never went out, while my mother often went out with two flasks to get water from some well.'

The arrival of the British army in August 1944 saw the Goldenbergs' subterranean ordeal come to an end, but it was not until 2010 that details of Bartali's actions emerged. The man was as modest as he was compassionate.

The end of the war saw Bartali return to professional cycling and he was soon back to his winning ways, triumphing at the 1946 Giro d'Italia before completing his second success at the Tour de France two years later. He died in 2000 at the age of 85, the end of a heroic and uplifting story, which is a wonderful testament to both altruism and pedal power.

TOEING THE LINE

FRANCE, 1947

It's no secret that riders of all eras have to make huge sacrifices to compete in the Tour de France. Racers put in countless hours of lonely training out on the roads and the agony of riding the Tour itself is legendary.

But few surely have made as big a sacrifice as the hapless French competitor Apo Lazarides, a man who took loyalty to a whole new level in 1947 when he received a rather onerous order from his team's lead rider.

The demanding 'grand fromage' in question was René Vietto, who had finished second in the 1939 Tour and was a notoriously fierce competitor and hardman. Potential disaster struck however during his preparations for the 1947 Tour, when a toe became infected with sepsis, and rather than miss the race, he ordered the doctor to amputate.

Vietto was, it seems, also a man who firmly believed in unity and after his operation he instructed Lazarides, his team 'domestique' or subordinate, to follow suit and get one of his own toes lopped off so that he might better understand the sacrifice required of Tour riders. He did as he was told and walked with a limp for the rest of his life as a result.

Dear old Apo actually had previous when it came to erratic behaviour in the race. 'Apo was an unusually impressionable fellow,' wrote Tim Moore in his book *French Revolutions: Cycling the Tour de France*. 'The year before [1946], leading the peloton by a county mile up the Izoard, he was seized by an imminent fear of attack by wild bears and stopped to wait for the rest to catch up.'

For the record, the nine-toed Vietto finished fifth in 1947 while the dutiful Lazarides, ahem, limped home in a reasonably respectable tenth. Legend has it that the more ghoulish cycling fan can view Vietto's toe perfectly preserved in a jar of formaldehyde behind the bar in a café in Marseilles. The fate of Apo's perfectly healthy toe is unknown, but it's unlikely he kept his discarded digit as a macabre memento of his painful Tour career.

CHICAGO DEFIES CONVENTION

USA, 1948

Almost as soon as the modern bicycle was born, forward-thinking enthusiasts armed with an alarming array of tools began to modify, adapt and generally pimp the classic design. Most of the mutated cycles that have resulted have served absolutely no practical purpose, but the devil makes work for idle hands and it's an essentially harmless hobby.

The first golden era of bike pimping came in the wake of the Second World War in the United States as our cousins across the pond grew weary of riding mundane, conventional cycles and decided to get to work in their garages. The epicentre of the craze was Chicago, and in true American style, what they produced was bigger and more bizarre than anything the cycling fraternity had seen before.

'To [the] Webster [dictionary] a bicycle is "a light vehicle having two wheels, one behind the other",' read an article in the December 1948 issue of *Time* magazine.

'Such a definition theoretically describes the contraptions but fails to do justice to the imagination of the Chicago chapter of the National Bicycle Dealers' Association.

'By artfully applying welders' torches to metal tubing, the chapter's members transform ordinary, utilitarian bicycles into travelling monstrosities.

'By far the most outlandish ideas have come from the Steinlauf family, who produced from their bicycle-repair shop most of the oddities. They are hazardous, generally at least one member of the clan is to be found in the hospital.'

Some of their creations – black-and-white pictures of which can be found with a cursory search of the World Wide Web – were certainly something to behold. A bike with square wheels was only the beginning for the Chicago innovators. They adapted the traditional concept of the tandem so that the two riders sat side by side rather than one in front of the other, and they also produced a five-seater bike. The bike with a series of metal spikes running on the outside of each wheel was even more surreal.

Their pièce de résistance, however, had to be what *Time* dubbed the 'Gangbuster Bike', a conventional tandem armed to the teeth with weapons. In total, it boasted 13 shotguns, two revolvers, six bayonets and even a flare gun – all mounted on the frame of the tandem – and, in Chicago at least, must have gone a long way to redressing the traditional pre-eminence of cars on the local roads.

BOYD'S BELGIAN BLUNDER

BELGIUM, 1950s

Local knowledge can be a precious if elusive commodity when you're racing far from home. Road races on foreign soil in particular can be a real test if you're not familiar with the street layout, and for this reason many a canny visiting cyclist has wisely chosen to stay on the wheels of one of the home-grown riders in the field to ensure they stay on course. It is not always a foolproof tactic, though, as this cautionary tale of wayward navigation proves.

We are in Belgium in the early 1950s and a Liverpudlian cyclist by the name of Pat Boyd has ventured over to Continental Europe to compete in a *kermesse*, a traditional town-based road race between 56 and 87 miles (90–140km) long and much favoured in the Flanders region of the country.

Unfortunately for Pat his European adventure did not go exactly according to plan. A puncture early in proceedings and the time taken to repair the damage meant he was way off the pace set by the leading group, and his hopes of a top ten finish already appeared distant.

He was, however, nothing if not a plucky rider, and with much huff and puff he managed to catch up with a Belgian cyclist towards the back of the pack, and the two stragglers began to work in tandem to reduce their collective deficit.

Their spirited fightback would probably still have been in vain had it not been for our aforementioned local knowledge and when Pat's new pal indicated an unassuming little alleyway, intimating that the secret shortcut was their only hope, the pair pedalled furiously down the passage. When they emerged at the other end of the alley, the peloton was suddenly and tantalisingly within sight. Pat was in business; he caught the leaders and remained in the pack for the rest of the race to register the top-ten finish he craved.

After the race our hero was all ready to buy his new Belgian friend a few beers by way of thanks, but he decided to keep his francs in his pocket when he realised that his new chum was actually a bit of a chump. The duo had indeed caught the leaders courtesy of their navigational naughtiness, but they had in fact caught the leaders of a completely separate *kermesse* race. As far as the organisers were concerned, the pair had finished last in *their* race.

Pat was not amused, and his humour was hardly improved when he arrived at Ostend and asked to be directed to the Liverpool ferry, only to find himself boarding a boat bound for Hull.

UPROAR OVER OSCAR
ITALY, 1950s

Cycling is essentially a non-contact sport. Obviously it's inevitable from time to time that an errant front wheel is going to accidentally come into contact with another rider and someone's going to take a spectacular tumble, but on the whole cyclists are gentle souls and prefer to pedal rather than punch their way to the finishing line.

They're not all angels though, and one rider renowned as more sinner than saint was Swiss rider Oscar Plattner, a sprinter who earned himself a reputation for his physical approach to racing. In short, if you got in Oscar's way he was more likely to go through rather than round you, and his abrasive tendencies saw him become one of the most frequently penalised cyclists on the European circuit during the 1950s.

We're not saying Oscar was a talented chap, but his elbows-first, excuses-later approach was very much in evidence when he was in Milan for one World Championship series event. He was competing against a local Italian lad and sure enough it wasn't long before the race witnessed liberal lashings of argy-bargy that enraged the predictably partisan crowd.

Both riders stormed into the judges' office to protest and counter-protest at the other's behaviour. The local rider was incandescent at Plattner's strong-arm tactics, while Oscar coldly invited him to come and have a go if he thought he was hard enough. After much deliberation, and doubtless eager to ensure their safe passage home from the velodrome, the officials ruled in favour of their compatriot.

Uncharacteristically, Oscar initially accepted their decision with barely a whimper but it turned out to be part of a cunning plan: the Swiss competitor merely waited for his 'victorious' rival to pack his bags and vacate the premises before lodging another complaint. With no one to mount a counter-argument, the judges reluctantly ruled in his favour and Oscar was told to head out onto the track, complete the 1,000m course and confirm his victory.

Oscar's Machiavellian manoeuvre appeared to have worked a treat, but he hadn't reckoned with the reaction of the Milanese crowd. Now we all know the Italians are usually a placid, undemonstrative bunch, but suffice to say they did not take kindly to Oscar's solo reappearance inside the velodrome, and as he attempted to complete the required distance, they pelted the scheming Swiss with fruit, bottles and any other projectile they could lay their hands on. After one too many vine-ripened plum tomatoes to the face, Oscar finally decided the time had come to say *arrivederci* to Milan and abandoned his attempt to finish the race.

Plattner died in 2002 but his muscular style of riding was not his only claim to fame. According to legend he was a 'big chap downstairs' (if you catch my drift), and his party trick was his disturbing ability to provide a fleshy perch for seven budgies. The only caveat was apparently that the seventh bird had to stand on one leg.

THE AUSSIES' UNLIKELY TANDEM TRIUMPH

FINLAND, 1952

It takes years of relentless sacrifice, unswerving dedication and gruelling training to win a coveted Olympic cycling gold. Only the strongest, fittest and fastest on two wheels get to stand on top of the podium before going on to star in adverts for energy drinks and breakfast cereals, or appear on *Strictly Come Dancing*.

That's the theory at least but there are exceptions to every rule, and the 1952 Games in Helsinki produced one of the most unlikely fairy tales in Olympic history, in the shape of Australian duo Lionel Cox and Russell Mockridge.

Our Antipodean pals headed to Finland to compete individually in the men's sprint race and 1,000m time trial respectively. Their arduous journey from down under took the Aussies via London and while they waited for their plane to Helsinki they bumped into a member of the British cycling team and got chatting.

After a wide-ranging conversation on Australia's constitutional relationship with the UK and the recent Ashes clash, the talk turned to the upcoming Olympic tandem race over 2,000m and high hopes of British success. The Australians hadn't entered the event but having hit it off in the departure lounge, the British rider gave Cox and Mockridge a spare track tandem, albeit disassembled and in need of much mechanical TLC.

The pair subsequently whipped out their spanners, wrenches and WD-40 and put the bike back together, a storeroom under the Olympic village serving as a makeshift workshop, and decided to enter the race on a whim. That they had never ridden together on a tandem was, in their opinion, no barrier to competing, while they agreed never to talk about the fact Cox had never actually pedalled a two-seater in his life. Hope obviously springs eternal down under.

They shouldn't have had a prayer, but on the day of the race the stars aligned, God was wearing a cork hat and Cox and Mockridge won gold, dramatically holding off the South African pairing of Raymond Robinson and Thomas Shardelow by a couple of inches in the home straight. 'Blokes who've trained on tandems for years wouldn't have done what we did, but we gave it a go,' Cox said some years after their triumph. 'We had one kick and a ride, and we gelled.'

It was certainly a great day for the duo. Mockridge also won gold in the 1,000m time trial, while Cox was second in the sprint, and both men headed home with double the number of medals they came for. Cox returned to his day job at a fruit and vegetable market in Sydney, while Mockridge continued riding before his tragic death six years later after a collision with a bus during a road race in Melbourne.

What our generous, unidentified British rider made of their success has sadly not been preserved for posterity. The Team GB tandem duo of Alan Bannister and Leslie Wilson finished a distant sixth in the race, and it's probably safe to assume our anonymous bike benefactor was in no rush to come forward after gifting Australia their unlikely victory.

AT ONE WITH NATURE
USA, 1954

The theme of discarded and forgotten childhood toys is one entertainingly explored in the *Toy Story* films, but sometimes real life is even more unbelievable than the big screen, as proven by the remarkable tale of Don Puz and his missing bicycle.

It was back in 1954 when the Puz family moved to Vashon Island in the state of Washington. Mrs Puz had been recently widowed and a generous member of the local community gave the family a children's cycle as a welcome present. It was a girl's bike but, Mrs Puz decided, it was exactly the right size for a then eight-year-old Don, and the poor lad had to suffer the considerable indignity of riding it around town.

Unsurprisingly it was not long before Don 'lost' the bike, and the family quickly forgot all about it.

Fast-forward to 2012 and Mrs Puz, now 99 years of age, is reading the local newspaper and notices a story about an old bike that has been discovered behind a local restaurant. Nothing unusual there until she reads on and learns that the cycle has been 'eaten' by a tree and is 5ft (1.5m) in the air.

A puzzled Mrs Puz and Don headed down to the eaterie for a look and after closer inspection confirmed that the bike was indeed the one that Don had abandoned more than half a century ago. He had left it propped up against the tree and over the intervening 58 years, the tree had grown up around the bike's frame, lifting it slowly but surely into the air as it matured.

It's an astonishing tale but the cherry on the cake was the revelation that the bike's front wheel, unencumbered by the trunk of the tree, still turned.

NOT A PRETTY PICTURE
AUSTRALIA, 1956

Britain's Olympic cycling adventure began in Athens back in 1896 (see 'All That Glitters is not Gold', page 39) and while the Games have rewarded us with plenty of thrills and spills, not to mention a flood of gold medals in recent years, British riders have not always enjoyed the best of luck at pivotal moments.

A desperately disappointing case in point occurred during the team road race at the 1956 Olympics in Melbourne, and underlined the fine and frequently ridiculous line between success and failure.

The three-man British team for the race consisted of Alan Jackson, the appropriately named Arthur Brittain and 20-year-old Yorkshireman Billy Holmes, and hopes were high our brave lads could become the Olympic champions.

Despite the searing temperature down under, everything was going according to plan until the 74⅔-mile (120km) point of the 116⅔-mile (188km) race, when young Holmes slowed down to grab a wet sponge from one of the race helpers and an over-eager photographer suddenly jumped into the road to take his picture. Billy never saw him coming and rider and idiotic snapper collided.

A few bumps and bruises weren't going to slow Billy down but his badly buckled front wheel inevitably did, and it took minutes to find a replacement. He lost valuable time on the leaders and limped over the line in fourteenth place.

Jackson came third and Brittain sixth, and had Holmes been able to come in twelfth or better, they would have edged out the French for gold. As it was they had to settle for silver and Billy was last spotted clutching a bicycle pump, whispering darkly about finding the offending snapper.

The whole race was a bit of a farce and the start was delayed when three Irish riders hijacked proceedings. The trio of Irish nationalists were not even supposed to be in Melbourne because they were members of the National Cycling Association of Ireland, a body not recognised by the International Cycling Union, but they somehow managed to conceal themselves among the field of 88 legitimate riders before causing chaos by shouting nationalist slogans and handing out pamphlets. The Aussie boys in blue were called and the ill-fated race could not start before the three protestors were hauled off in handcuffs.

The controversy did not end there, and there were squeals of protest from both Britain and France after Italian rider Ercole Baldini crossed the finishing line first, both teams claiming he had deliberately ridden the final stages of the race sandwiched between two film trucks to unfairly shield himself from the wind. The complaints were dismissed but the sense of anger either side of the Channel was, at best, thinly disguised.

To cap a thoroughly chaotic day, the tape recorder with the national anthems failed to work during the medal presentation ceremony and Team GB left in silence, vowing to run over the next photographer stupid enough to cross their path.

UNBEATABLE BERYL
ENGLAND, 1959

The exhilarating exploits of Victoria Pendleton, Lizzie Armitstead, Emma Pooley, Laura Trott *et al* in recent years has seen the profile of women's cycling in Britain rise to unprecedented, dizzy heights. The fairer sex have been looking sharper in the saddle than the heels on a pair of Manolo Blahniks lately.

The godmother of women's cycling in Blighty, however, has to be the late, great Beryl Burton, a lady who redefined the meaning of sporting domination and whose longevity would make the Duracell bunny blush.

Born in Leeds in 1937, she was introduced to the joys of cycling by her husband Charlie and in 1957 she won silver at the national individual time-trial championship. It was to prove merely the beginning of a truly phenomenal career.

Our Beryl proceeded to wipe the floor with the opposition. 'No other British sportswoman has dominated their field in the way that Beryl Burton dominated the world of cycling,' read her obituary in *The Independent* following her death in 1996. 'As *Velo Gotha*, the Belgian bible of cycling facts and figures succinctly puts it:

"She was the best known and most successful woman cyclist".

'In the course of a career that spanned five decades, the fiercely competitive Yorkshirewoman won seven world titles – two road race championships and five track pursuit titles – and 96 national titles – 12 road race championships, 13 pursuit titles and 71 time trial titles against the clock.'

These considerable achievements were only the tip of the iceberg, though, and Beryl is perhaps best and most fondly remembered for two iconic feats.

The first occurred in 1967 when she set a new national record of 277 miles (446km) in a 12-hour time trial. That in itself would have been impressive enough, but in setting the record Beryl overtook Mike McNamara – who was in the process of setting the men's 12-hour record – and according to legend impudently offered Mike a Liquorice Allsort, which he sheepishly accepted. For two years, Beryl's 277-mile mark was a record for any British cyclist, male or female.

Her other great claim to fame was her remarkable record in, deep breath now, the Road Time Trials Council's British Best All-Rounder competition, a convoluted way of describing the process of finding the best overall rider in the country.

Beryl was first crowned champion in 1959 and for 25 consecutive years she remained unbeaten and unbowed, claiming her last title in 1984. That's an unblemished quarter of a century as champion. It's also worth noting Beryl was an amateur, a proud housewife and occasional fruit picker and worker in the rhubarb farms in Yorkshire, and training and competing had to be balanced with family life.

She died young, at the age of just 58, but she left an indelible mark on her beloved sport. Awarded an MBE in 1964 and made an OBE four years later, her life was celebrated in 2012 in a Radio 4 play entitled *Beryl: A Love Story on Two Wheels*, an epitaph that says it all.

AU REVOIR, MONSIEUR LE PRESIDENT

FRANCE, 1960

Etiquette can be a problematic convention. One man's due deference can be another man's discourtesy, and unless someone explains the rules, it's remarkably easy for protocol to fall victim to confusion and ignorance.

And so it was on the penultimate stage of the 1960 Tour de France from Besançon to Troyes, when the organisers unexpectedly learned that a rather important spectator would be watching the race. The VIP in question was none less than the French President, General de Gaulle, who, they were told, would be at the bottom of his garden in the village of Colombey-les-Deux-Églises near Troyes to cheer the peloton through.

The Tour director Jacques Goddet hit on the idea of an impromptu tribute to the hugely popular President, and quickly located French national champion Henry Anglade to discuss his thoughts on the hoof.

'We were right at the end of the Tour, the day before we finished in Paris,' Anglade recalled. 'I was at the back of the bunch when Jacques Goddet came up alongside me. He said, "We've just learned that General de Gaulle is at Colombey. Would it be an inconvenience if the race stopped to greet him?" I said to him, "You're asking all the riders to stop in full flight?"'

The experienced Anglade realised the dangers of the peloton coming to a dangerously abrupt halt en masse and began to forewarn his fellow competitors what was about to happen.

'I went back up to the head of the race to talk to the team leaders and then I dropped back down the bunch telling the other riders as they passed,' he said. 'Finally I dropped back to the race director's car to say that the riders had all agreed.'

The race entered Colombey at a sedate pace and then ground to an even more sedate stop outside de Gaulle's garden without destroying a single petunia. Pleasantries between some of the peloton's leading lights and the President were exchanged, and Goddet's PR stunt appeared to have worked a treat.

That was until Frenchman Pierre Beuffeuil finally reached Colombey. The Centre-Midi team rider saw his dismounted rivals by the side of the road but rather than join them, he pedalled furiously onwards to Troyes. The peloton were absolutely flabbergasted but despite their frantic chase, they could not catch Beuffeuil and he claimed a shock stage victory.

The sting in the tail is it was not Beuffeuils' fault. He had suffered a puncture earlier in the stage and had spent most of the day playing catch-up. The message about the collective pause in proceedings had never reached him and he was certainly none the wiser when he suddenly came across his fellow riders taking time off.

Goddet wanted Beuffeuil charged with treason but when it was pointed out France was a republic rather than a constitutional monarchy, he knew he'd never make it stick.

CYCLING ON THE CURRICULUM

USA, 1961

In the UK, learning to ride safely used to be taught in school via the medium of the Cycling Proficiency Test. Introduced in October 1947, the CPT essentially involved swerving around a few judiciously placed obstacles in the playground and if you managed not to fall off, run over the tester's toes or maim the school guinea pig, you tended to pass.

The CPT has been replaced by the irritatingly modern 'Bikeability' scheme, but the theory remains essentially the same. If you can get from A to B on two wheels with the minimum number of civilian casualties en route, you're in.

In the States, of course, they do things differently, and when the St Helens School in Ohio was opened in 1961, the new headmaster decided unicycling would become a mandatory subject, reasoning it would be an engaging way to encourage physical education. The pupils were supplied with bikes and the school began to forge itself a bizarre reputation as the seat of learning of choice for those who liked pedalling on one wheel.

It was not long, however, before the unusual curriculum choice began to help swell the school's coffers. 'Unicycles have become the rage and trademark of one school, St Helen Parish School in Newbury, Ohio,' reported *The Tuscaloosa News* in an article in September 1970. 'Cycles are ridden by all of its 97 pupils. They're famous and their prowess has proven a profitable thing for the school. Teams of the best riders have been guests in Macy's parade and on national television variety shows and the school has won a contract from Goodyear to test the company's bike tyres.'

They also performed at the Inaugural Parade for Jimmy Carter as president in 1977, the Rose Bowl and World's Fair and it was not long before anxious prospective parents were actually paying to have their kids privately tutored in the art of unicycling to ensure they got into the school.

Sadly, the appetite for the school's unique sporting activity slowly waned and by the early 1990s, unicycling in the corridors was no more. There was, though, a 2013 reunion for the alumni of 1965–85 as past pupils pedalled their way down memory lane.

THE IDIOCY OF INERTIA
JAPAN, 1965

Albert Einstein was a very clever man. The Nobel Prize winner's revolutionary theory of relativity remains one of the two central pillars of modern physics, his $E = mc^2$ formula is one of the most famous in the world and he could finish *The Times* sudoku without breaking into a sweat.

He also knew a thing or two about bikes. 'Life is like riding a bicycle,' he wrote in a letter to his 20-year-old son Eduard in 1930. 'To keep your balance you must keep moving.' Wise words from Albert there, but advice that Japanese Tsugunobu Mitsuishi decided to completely disregard when he set out to break one of cycling's most pointless records imaginable.

The nature of Mitsuishi's challenge? To remain completely stationary on a cycle without falling off for as long as possible. No pedalling, no forward motion, no tippy toes on the floor – just balancing on an untethered bike without keeling over.

The 39-year-old Tokyo man embarked on his quest back in 1965 and, ignoring the heated debate about whether deliberately remaining motionless wasn't rather against the spirit of cycling, he managed to stay upright for a remarkable five hours and 25 minutes straight. Mitsuishi may have been a nutter but you've got to admire his poise.

Mercifully, his magnificent immobility appears to have discouraged anyone from attempting to surpass his milestone. There are no records of legitimate challenges to his bizarre record but further research does reveal there was one unnamed lady who thought she'd have a half-hearted shot at the title.

Sadly she didn't quite get to grips with the basic rules of the game, as *Guinness World Records* co-founder Ross McWhirter revealed in an interview ten years after Mitsuishi's soporific feat.

'There was a woman who demanded to be put in the book because she had sat on a stationary bicycle longer than anyone,' McWhirter explained. 'It turned out she had gone to a bicycle shop and sat on a bicycle with clamps and so on to hold it up. Whereas Tsugunobu Mitsuishi had balanced on a real bicycle. So I said to her, after all, you have to compare like with like. And she still kept writing letters.'

For anyone else contemplating an attempt to eclipse Mitsuishi's surreal achievement, exercise bikes don't count either.

THE WHITE BIKE MAN
HOLLAND, 1965

You can barely move for 'Boris Bikes' in London these days. At the last count there were 8,000 of them in the capital, and although the city has not yet become the Mecca for pedestrians and cyclists alike that some envisaged since the scheme's introduction in the summer of 2010, motorists can definitely detect the wind of change.

Unsurprisingly there's been a bit of a barney about who takes credit for the aforementioned sharing scheme. The rent-on-the-spot idea came to fruition during Boris Johnson's first term as London Mayor, but it was his predecessor, Ken Livingstone, who originally floated the big idea back in 2008. The two politicians have been bickering over who gets the credit like squabbling schoolboys ever since.

The real mastermind behind the scheme, however, has to be the fabulously named Laurens Maria Hendrikus Schimmelpennink, or Luud Schimmelpennink if you can't quite get your tongue round his full title, who pioneered the concept of free city cycling over in Holland in the 1960s.

Clever Luud was a member of the Provo movement in Amsterdam, a freethinking radical group whose mission statement was to shake things up a bit. In July 1965 they published a pamphlet entitled 'Provocation No. 5' in which they advocated the use of free bikes to alleviate Amsterdam's congestion and pollution problems.

As usual, the Establishment was too busy enjoying their G&Ts and going to the opera to actually do anything, so Schimmelpennink and his chums assembled ten or so bikes, painted them all white and simply left them around the city for anyone to use whenever they fancied. The embryonic 'White Bicycle Plan' was born.

Unfortunately, the long arm of the law was not happy and they ruled that leaving an unlocked bike on the streets of the capital was an offence. They heartlessly confiscated the lot.

'The plan was to stop the car, the destruction of the town, the pollution, by leaving cars outside the town and give a new instrument for people to use when they want to travel around,' Schimmelpennink explained in a recent interview.

'Free bikes, for everybody. But the police took them away, of course, in their feeling it was not allowed to put a bike without lock. The point was we were not making a system at that moment, we were making an idea.

'In the minds of the politicians, bikes were a thing of the past. In their opinion, the future was through the car. But they were wrong. We know that now in this moment, bikes are the future, and the car will be changed. It was a very powerful idea.'

Schimmelpennink was not beaten yet and adhered to the old mantra 'if you can't beat them, join them', winning election to the Municipal Council of the City of Amsterdam in early 1967 with the ambition of making the 'White Bicycle Plan' a reality.

He proposed flooding the city with 10,000 publicly funded bikes and although his ambitious plan was blocked by political opponents, you cannot kill an idea, and after a long period of germination, community bicycle schemes began to emerge in cities throughout Europe and North America.

Unlike Boris Johnson in London, Schimmelpennink never saw his name colloquially attached to the Amsterdam initiative, which was probably for the best in the interests of brevity.

OUT OF THIS WORLD

USA, 1973

According to Captain James T. Kirk in *Star Trek*, his mission was 'to boldly go where no man has gone before'. It was a brave attitude that got him and his Federation chums on the *Enterprise* into a few tight corners – not least the sacrificial lamb that invariably got killed when they beamed down onto an alien planet each week – but you've still got to admire his sense of adventure.

It was exactly this real-life pioneering spirit that was the catalyst for the American Moon landings and, in due course, resulted in the first ever bicycle ride in space. Beat that, William Shatner.

The watershed moment came in 1973 during the Skylab 3 mission to the first American space station, Skylab. Three astronauts blasted off from the Kennedy Space Centre in Florida and once they'd successfully docked with the station, they began a series of medical experiments.

The commander of the mission was Alan Bean, and although he already held the distinction as the fourth man to walk on the Moon after flying on the Apollo 12 mission four years earlier, far greater fame beckoned when he became the first man to jump into the saddle outside the Earth's atmosphere.

To be clear, Bean did not actually disengage the air locks, pop on a suit and pedal out into the cold, dark abyss that is space. He was safely seated on a stationary bike inside the station, hooked up to all manner of gadgets and computers, and spent 90 minutes or so pedalling away to assess how he coped physically in the unique, gravity-free conditions. Bean, however, did have a novel way of timing his ride, eschewing his watch and instead pedalling for the time it took Skylab to make a complete orbit of the Earth.

BMX
GETS A 'BUM' DEAL
1974

For some snooty cycling purists, the BMX will forever be regarded as the black sheep of the two-wheeled family. To them it's an unruly and unkempt cousin that's just too loud and too brash for polite society. For everyone else, it's an absolute riot.

The stuffy traditionalists' attempts to give bicycle motocross the cold shoulder suffered a major blow in 2008 when it made its Olympic debut at the Beijing Games. The long fight for recognition and legitimacy was over and BMX had finally been accepted by its peers.

That battle for equal billing began in the States in 1970 when Scot Breithaupt, the undisputed godfather of BMX, organised the first ever 'official' race on a dirt track in California. The popularity of the sport exploded almost overnight and Breithaupt had a phenomenon on his hands.

There was, though, one minor fly in the ointment – Breithaupt decided to call his burgeoning new set-up the Bicycle United Motocross Society. That's B.U.M.S. to you and me.

'I used to race motorcross and when I practiced local kids would come out and imitate my jumps,' Breithaupt explained. 'The original BMX track was 'B.U.M.S. I' in Long Beach in California. It was gnarly. It was a trail that I used for practice on my motorcycle. I rode for the Yamaha factory as a support rider. The track was about 450 yards

(411m) long and we ran two laps. It had a 35ft (10.7m) high drop-away jump, a mud hole and eight or nine other jumps.'

Despite its ridiculous acronym, the new umbrella group for BMXers flourished in the early 1970s and Breithaupt was organising bigger and bolder events.

'By 1974 I promoted the Yamaha Bicycle Gold Cup Series and had over 1,000 riders at each event,' he said. 'We held the finals in the LA Coliseum. About 16,000 spectators were there, which is probably the biggest event ever to this day. It was huge.'

Exactly a decade later the same venue staged the opening ceremony of the Los Angeles Olympics, and although it was to be a further 24 years before a BMX was pedalled at the Games in Beijing, bicycle motocross was by then firmly on its way to getting a proper job, a sensible haircut and pension plan.

LUCK OF THE IRISH RUNS OUT

SOUTH AFRICA, 1975

Politics and sport have rarely made for happy bedfellows, but the sporting boycott of South Africa during the Apartheid era was an exception to the rule, a powerful statement of intent to the country's white rulers that the world would no longer tolerate their racist regime.

There were sanctions for those sportsmen and women who chose to ignore the boycott, and the threat of suspension or a long ban led to all sorts of clandestine incidents as those who did travel to South Africa to compete went to great lengths to remain anonymous.

One such tale involved the Irish riders Pat McQuaid, who had recently won the Tour of Ireland, and Sean Kelly, the national junior champion, who accepted an invitation to compete in the 1975 instalment of the Rapport Tour between Cape Town and Johannesburg. Cycling's world body the Union Cycliste Internationale (UCI) had turned its back on South Africa five years earlier, and both men knew they'd be in hot water indeed if details of their trip were to be made public.

They made it to South Africa undetected and, racing under false names, it seemed they'd get away with it. That was until Elizabeth Taylor and Richard Burton unexpectedly made an appearance.

The famed Hollywood couple had just tied the knot for the second time and as part of their honeymoon, they arrived in

Oudtshoom in the Western Cape for a stopover at exactly the same time McQuaid and Kelly and the Rapport Tour were also in town.

A local reporter noticed there was a 'British' team listed as taking part in the race and asked the manager whether he could organise a publicity picture with his riders and Taylor and Burton. The wheels were about to come off McQuaid and Kelly's subterfuge.

The team manager tried to pull the wool over the reporter's eyes by putting up a selection of local riders in place of the Irish boys but the ruse failed to throw him off the scent and, after a bit of digging, he discovered the true identities of the racers.

'The secret team who masquerade as Britain,' ran the headline after the journalist sold the story to the *Daily Mail*, and McQuaid and Kelly suddenly found themselves exposed.

The UCI were not amused and both men were banned for six months. Worse was to follow though when the UCI forwarded their names to the International Olympic Committee, who imposed lifetime bans on both and dashed their dreams of riding at the 1976 Games in Montreal.

Taylor and Burton divorced for a second time in 1976, presumably blissfully unaware of the impact their short-lived marriage had had on Irish cycling.

The controversy, though, clearly didn't ruin McQuaid's long-term prospects, rising through the ranks as he did to become the president of the UCI in 2006, a perplexing example of the poacher becoming the extremely well-remunerated gamekeeper.

THE BREAKAWAY THAT BACKFIRED
FRANCE, 1978

There's an old saying that 'some rules are meant to be broken' but when it comes to the Tour de France, some unwritten rules are definitely sacrosanct. In particular, the convention that states that the peloton is a democracy rather than a free-for-all. The consequences for ignoring this can be severe, as naive French rider Dante Coccolo found to his cost during the 1978 Tour.

The incident occurred on a gruelling 130-mile (209km) stage from Bordeaux to Biarritz. It was a hot day, the 100-strong field had been taking on plenty of liquids and it was not long before some of the riders felt the inevitable call of nature. The collective cry for a comfort break went up and 30 or so competitors dashed behind the nearest bush.

The rest of the peloton did the decent thing and slowed down. All, that is, except for Coccolo, who cheekily decided to speed up and try to build a significant if ill-gotten lead. It was a flagrant breach of protocol and a move he would quickly come to regret.

'He had a habit of attacking on bathroom breaks,' explained Paul Sherwen, a British rider who was in the peloton that day. 'He thought it was quite amusing. It's not illegal but if 20 or 30 guys stop for a break and you go off on an attack, you're going to make 20 or 30 enemies.'

'When it was Coccolo's turn for his own bathroom break and he put his bike down on the grass verge, a couple of guys slowed down and grabbed the bike. They wheeled it down the road for a kilometre or two and tossed it into a ditch. Everyone in the peloton was very happy about it.'

The dastardly Coccolo was now stranded and had to wait for five minutes before his Jobo-Spidel team car arrived to take him to locate his missing bike. He had to ride on the bonnet of the car, an ignominious end to a less than edifying day. The conniving Frenchman went on to finish second last in that year's Tour and never competed in the race again. He was not sorely missed by his fellow riders.

THE MARVEL OF MUNI

CANADA, 1980s

Close your eyes and think of a unicycle. The odds are you're now picturing an oversized, one-wheeled bike with a clown perched precariously in the saddle; or a juggler; or maybe a clown juggling – inside a big top.

The point here is that the much-maligned unicycle has often been dismissed as little more than the Mr Bean of the bicycle family, good for a laugh from time to time but not a machine with any serious merit.

Some cyclists do not subscribe to such a dismissive view of the modest one-wheeler. Some, in fact, fervently maintain that two wheels are for squares, and if you know where to look, there are plenty of serious unicycling race meetings – there's not a red nose or custard pie in sight – not to mention versions of basketball, handball and hockey, with the players proudly propelling themselves around on a single circle of rubber.

The most extreme and unlikely deployment of the machine, however, has to be the bizarre but courageous sport of mountain unicycling, also known as muni, which sees riders pedalling their merry way up and down hill and dale and, apparently, not falling off nearly as much as you might imagine.

Muni began in the 1980s when a small band of intrepid mountain bikers hit on the idea of spicing up their usual routes by losing a wheel. After a few initial bumps and bruises, it became apparent that the humble unicycle (albeit modified and rather beefed up) was just as capable of going up the same steep ascents and down equally scary descents as its two-wheeled cousins, and ever since Muni has been going from strength to strength.

'Unicycling is challenging to learn, but not difficult once you know how,' said Canadian Kris Holm, one of the sport's pioneers and the author of *The Essential Guide to Mountain and Trials Unicycling*. 'So above all, be patient with yourself. Most riders take 10–15 hours to learn the basics. Although at first intimidating, it is surprisingly easy to get started. In fact, if you can ride down the street, you already have the skills to start mountain unicycling.

'Originally I was inspired by a street performer and asked for a unicycle for my twelfth birthday. That was in 1986. I didn't know anyone else who rode one, and coming from an outdoorsy family, it just seemed natural to ride on single track. I was also into rock climbing and trials unicycling.

'I'd take my unicycle to a local beach and try to ride on rocks and logs but it wasn't until much later that this time period became known as the origins of mountain and trials unicycling.

'Just like bikes, you can start riding easy trails as soon as you can ride down the street. Even though you fall more, it's actually safer than mountain biking because top speeds are lower. The most basic off-road riding skill you need is to ride while holding the front saddle handle, for control over rocks and bumps.'

Details of the number of active mountain unicyclists are hard to come by but it is probably no coincidence that as circuses have suffered a 21st-century slump in popularity, Muni's ranks have been swelled by new recruits with surprisingly bouffant red hair and a penchant for face paint.

HOY'S DEBT TO HOLLYWOOD

SCOTLAND, 1982

It was definitely a mixed year at the movies back in 1982. On the one hand, cinemagoers were able to feast their eyes on cult classics *Blade Runner* and *Tron*, the epic *Gandhi* and acclaimed romantic drama *An Officer and a Gentleman*. On the other hand they could, if they were injudicious in their ticket purchases, find themselves subjected to *Porky's*, *The Thing* or *The Slumber Party Massacre*. If they were really unlucky, they might have even had to sit through *Annie*.

The most successful film of the year however was Steven Spielberg blockbuster *ET the Extra-Terrestrial*, the touching tale of a young boy who befriends an alien stranded on Earth. It was a film that made Spielberg millions and irritatingly ensured the phrase 'phone home' was never far from every wag's lips.

More pertinently considering the theme of this book, it was also the movie directly responsible for Great Britain winning six Olympic cycling medals. For it was back in 1982 that a fresh-faced primary school kid from Edinburgh persuaded his dad to take him to the pictures to watch the film, and British cycling would never be the same again. The young chap, of course, was Chris Hoy.

'I was watching *ET* when I was about six years of age and I'd never seen a BMX bike before,' Hoy admitted in 2013 when he announced his retirement. 'It's the scene at the end of the film when they're getting chased by the police.

I just thought, wow, I'd like to give that a go. The BMX scenes were fantastic, so I pestered my dad into taking me along to the local track at Danderhall where I saw all these kids having terrific fun. That was it. I was hooked and it all sort of spiralled from there.'

The rest, as they say, is history. Hoy won his first gold at the Athens Olympics in 2004 in the 1km (1,000-yard) time trial, a wonderful hat-trick of titles at the Games in Beijing and, finally, gold in both the Team Sprint and Keirin at the Velodrome at the 2012 Olympic Games in London in the climax to a glittering career.

Spielberg did rather well too after *ET* but while Hoy's career was without blemish, the American did blot his copybook when he produced *An American Tail: Fievel Goes West* in 1991 and directed *The Adventures of Tintin* 20 years later. Celluloid crimes for which we can probably forgive him after inspiring the most successful Olympian British cycling has ever produced.

MORGAN'S BEASTLY LEAP

USA, 1982

They say elephants never forget. It's never been made entirely clear why we imbue the big fellas with such good memories but it's probably safe to assume the nine African bull elephants who were corralled in a car park in Illinois back in 1982 never forgot their unusual day out.

Circus elephants, of course, are no strangers to showbiz, but our nine intrepid beasts had never seen anything like it as John 'Mercury' Morgan proceeded to successfully jump over all of them on a bright yellow bicycle. The stunt was part of a short-lived American TV show called *That's Incredible!* and Morgan's nine-animal feat, a leap of some 50ft (15.2m), remains a world record for a bike jumping over elephants. Admittedly, it's not the most hotly contested of categories in the *Guinness Book of World Records*, but it's easy to mock.

Morgan's fascinating career as a stunt rider began in the 1970s when his mum refused to buy him a motorbike and his dreams of emulating Evel Knievel were cruelly dashed. It was pedal power or nothing for him, and after practising flying over rubbish bins on his bike, he graduated up to leaping over cars and jumping through rings of fire. You know, the usual stuff.

The elephant stunt was inspired by his love of the circus and once he'd persuaded the producers of *That's Incredible!* that it would make great television, he got the green light. You can still watch footage of the jump on the web, although you are forewarned that his yellow jumpsuit isn't exactly easy on the eye and there is the small fact he needs a tow from a motorbike to reach the required speed to make the leap and avoid leaving tyre marks on the back of a disgruntled 15,000lb (6,804kg) animal.

A few years later, Morgan fulfilled his dream of working in the circus when he was taken on by the Ringling Bros. and Barnum & Bailey Circus. The angry and suspicious looks from the circus elephants on his first day told their own story.

INTO THE
VALLEY OF DEATH
USA, 1983

According to Alfred, Lord Tennyson's famous Crimean War poem 'The Charge of the Light Brigade', it was the 600 who recklessly rode 'into the valley of Death'. To be fair they were only obeying orders, but only half of them made it back in one piece and it wasn't the smartest move ever.

The two-wheeled equivalent of the infamous British charge must surely be the Furnace Creek 508 race in America. For Valley of Death read the Death Valley desert, for 600 cavalry read 250 cyclists and for insanely ill-advised read, well, insanely ill-advised.

First staged in 1983, the Furnace Creek 508 bills itself as the 'toughest 48 hours in sport', and when you take a closer look at the route riders must follow to complete the gruelling 508-mile (818km) race, it's very hard to disagree.

Competitors begin in the salubrious surroundings of Santa Clarita, 25 miles (40.2km) north of Los Angeles, and must pedal across Death Valley before finishing in the marvellously named town of Twentynine Palms. The halfway point takes the cyclists through Furnace Creek in the desert (hence the name) where, fact fans, a staggering record air temperature of 134°F (56.7°C) was recorded back in 1913. Which is seriously hot.

Riders have 48 hours to complete the crazy course – first across the line wins – but if the desert and the extreme heat weren't enough to contend with, the route is also far from flat. In fact, it rises and falls so dramatically that completing the 508 means competitors are riding the equivalent of four mountain stages of the Tour de France back-to-back.

Unsurprisingly, only about 60 per cent of entrants in the individual race actually complete the course, but mercifully for them, unlike the poor sods in the Charge of the Light Brigade, they simply retire from the race rather than get blown to pieces by Russian cannons.

A brutal event the 508, then, but it does boast one endearing, rather cuddly feature. Competitors in the race are not identified by numbers but rather by 'totems', animal-based nicknames, which they can choose themselves or are assigned by the organisers.

Past individual and relay competitors have gone for totems such as 'Chesapeake Bay Retriever', 'Raven Lunatics', 'Relucent Phoenix' and 'Pudu and the Pussycats', but the award for the least confidence-inspiring choice has to go to the rider who elected to be called the 'Banana Slug'.

THE GREAT GLOBAL DASH

AROUND THE WORLD, 1984

It was dear old Thomas Stevens (see 'The Amazing Travels of Thomas', page 25) who first contemplated the insanity that is pedalling around the world, and ever since his successful circumnavigation back in 1886, deranged riders and cracked cyclists have been attempting to emulate his groundbreaking feat.

It took Thomas two years and nine months to complete his remarkable journey. To be fair, he enjoyed some extremely generous and leisurely stopovers along the way, but back then simply getting from A to B (and eventually all the way back to A again) rather than sheer speed was the main priority.

Ever since 1984, however, his spiritual successors have been all about the pace as they've battled for the coveted title of the Guinness World Records fastest circumnavigation of the globe, a challenge so ridiculously arduous that it really should come with a health warning, a big scary skull and crossbones and 'Police Line Do Not Cross' tape.

The first to set a verified time was Brit Nick Sanders in 1984, who pedalled a 13,000-mile (20,921km) route across the northern hemisphere in 78 days. His verified record stood until 2003, when GWR suddenly changed the rules to require challengers to cover 24,900 miles (40,072km), which includes the unavoidable ocean crossings by air or boat, via two antipodal points and, rather harshly, Sanders' efforts were summarily expunged from the record books.

Since then, many have tried and most have failed to set a new milestone, but Mike Hall was successful in 2012 when he set off from the Royal Observatory in Greenwich in June, returning to the same spot a staggering 91 days and 18 hours later.

Hall averaged roughly 200 miles (322km) a day on a journey which took him through 20 countries and four continents and it was patently obvious when he arrived back in London that the trip had nearly beaten him.

'I think I had a lot of the emotions in the last few weeks on the roads,' he said after crossing the finishing line. 'It was quite difficult and I think it builds up, the stress. So I kind of released all that in the last few days.

'There's been some moments, some kind of breakdowns, but I keep the breakdowns on the bike. I don't stop for those. I broke my bike [in Albania] but managed to fix it with some parts I had, and then had to ride through the night to get to Greece. There were a few close calls with traffic but I just tried to keep safe, keep vigilant.'

Hall's fragile mood did not improve a few weeks later. In their infinite wisdom, the good people at GWR decided to change their record-setting criteria once again, and decreed that the time spent in the air or on the sea had to be added to the time actually spent in the saddle and Hall's journey time was recalculated to 107 days, two hours and 30 minutes. In December 2012 German Thomas Großerichter came home in 105 days, one hour and 44 minutes.

In 2013 GWR announced yet another change in their rules, which ordained that the time spent waiting for rather than just travelling on the assorted planes, trains and automobiles (OK, not automobiles) required to complete the trip, now had to be added to the total. Remarkably, at the time of going to press, for once the rules of the great global dash had remained unchanged.

The current holder of the coveted title of 'fastest global pedaller' is New Zealander Andrew Nicholson. A former speed skater, who represented his country at three Winter Olympic Games, Andrew set off from Auckland airport in August 2015 and after 123 days and 43 minutes in the saddle he was back on the same stretch of runway.

Rumours that GWR were going to chalk off Andrew's effort just because that was just their thing thankfully proved unfounded.

'LOOK, NO HANDS!'

ITALY, 1985

For many cyclists, true happiness is simply finding the right stretch of road on which to pedal. Whether it's a stunning coastal route, a picturesque rural B-road or a woodland path through the flora and fauna, cycling is an experience which can be significantly enhanced by the right surroundings.

Mountainous routes also tend to be popular despite the exertion required to get to the top. The panoramic views, the invariably twisting tarmac and the sense of sheer escape can make an elevated road irresistible. If you live in the hills, you've got no choice anyway.

One of the most spectacular mountain routes in the world is the breathtaking Stelvio Pass in Italy. It lies in the Eastern Alps and its highest point is 9,042ft (2,757m) above sea level, but what really makes it special are the 48 hairpin bends that lie before the descending rider as he or she nervously navigates the way down.

From the air, the road looks like a petulant child has angrily thrown a few strands of spaghetti at the mountainside, and cyclists adore the Stelvio's complexity and whiff of danger.

But while most are content to work their way cautiously up and down, local boy Giuliano Calore likes to spice things up, and over the years the Italian has attempted and completed a series of mind-blowing stunts on the mountain.

Anticipating the antics of German Christian Adam (see 'Onward Christian Soloist', page 119), Calore ascended the Stelvio in 1981 playing in turn four different musical instruments, climaxing with an amplified accordion. In 1986 he climbed all 9,042ft of the mountain in a time of 2 hours and 20 minutes while it was covered in snow and the temperature was 14°F (-10°C). Three years later he got to the top once again but this time on a bike lacking both handlebars and brakes.

His undisputed pièce de résistance, however, came in 1985 when he sat at the top of the pass seated on another bicycle devoid of both brakes and handlebars. All 48 of the Stelvio's terrifying hairpins hungrily awaited him but Calore refused to back down and set off downwards.

He averaged 50mph (80km/h) on the descent, successfully negotiating all the potentially disastrous corners, and just 27 minutes later, he was safely at the bottom having conquered the Stelvio without the luxury of either brakes or steering.

ONWARD CHRISTIAN SOLOIST

1988

The Germans, as a rule, are not renowned for their madcap sense of humour. They've got the whole car-manufacturing gig sorted and they're world leaders when it comes to fiscal responsibility, but there's a reason why there has never been a Teutonic version of *You've Been Framed*.

Which is, of course, an extremely lazy national stereotype and one which was comprehensively debunked in the 1980s by Christian Adam and his one-man quest to combine his love of music and cycling.

A classically trained violinist, Adam was looking for a new challenge and decided riding his bicycle backwards while knocking out a few tunes on his instrument was the next logical step. He would wear his coat and tails for the occasion, he would attach his sheet music to the seat and he would steer the bike while sitting on the handlebars with his bum.

What could possibly go wrong? His first attempt, in 1987, to set a new world record for cycling backwards while playing the violin – a record no one is convinced actually existed before Adam's bizarre effort – was a humdinger, and he clocked up 37½ miles (60.5km) in a time of five hours and nine minutes.

According to Adam, he played J.S. Bach for most of the journey, and was particularly impressed with the acoustics he encountered in a motorway tunnel. His second shot, in

1988, did not go as smoothly as the first, although by now Adam was clearly getting the hang of the whole reverse cycling challenge and covered a remarkable 70¼ miles (113km) in just under six hours.

The problem was the very abrupt end to the ride as he collided with a cycling policeman and both men ended up in a rather undignified heap. Luckily for Adam, the dazed copper decided to overlook the myriad of traffic laws he was probably breaking with his silly shenanigans, but he did make him pay for the repair of his bike.

With rivals wanting to challenge Adam conspicuous by their absence, there are no further reports of him trying to extend his absurd record.

'ST MICHAEL'
TO THE RESCUE
FRANCE, 1990

Lengthy lunch breaks, extra-marital affairs and an innate distrust of the English are as French as the Eiffel Tower. Throw in angry farmers with a political axe to grind and you've virtually got the definition of the French way of life.

French farmers simply love to protest. It's part of the job description, and they were in particularly militant mood in 1990 as the wholesale price of their lamb plummeted. The Union Paysanne, the farmers' union, blamed the Government, the Common Agricultural Policy and cheap imports for the drop, and there was much muttering and cursing throughout the countryside.

The 1990 Tour de France presented our disgruntled farmers with the perfect opportunity to protest publicly, and they'd already got their retaliation in first, disrupting the first day's riding by scattering branches, straw bales and diesel oil along the route.

It was, though, day four, and the 144-mile (232km), rather rural stage from Poitiers to Nantes that was the real worry. Angry farmers could and probably would be hiding behind every hedge and as the peloton began to pedal slowly out of Poitiers that morning, race director Jean Marie Leblanc was an understandably nervous man.

His anxiety was justified and reports quickly began to filter through that the dreaded agricultural protesters had gathered just outside the village of Sainte-Gemme, 50 miles (80km) from Poitiers, and were in confrontational mood. Trees had been felled by the side of the road, tyres had been set alight, and there were far too many freshly sharpened pitchforks for comfort.

Leblanc had a decision to make and ordered the riders to stop a few miles short of St-Gemme. It looked like the farmers had won.

They hadn't, however, reckoned with a local teenager by the name of Michael who, according to legend, was appalled by their protest and the unwelcome notoriety it was bringing to his village.

Michael jumped on his little 50cc bike and invited the peloton to follow him on the back roads, bypassing the blockage. The riders accepted and for a surreal 32km (19.9 miles) before they all rejoined the original route, the Tour was led through the French countryside by a teenager on a scooter.

The farmers were furious, but since their tractors didn't have the pace to catch the peloton, there was absolutely nothing they could do about it.

MARIO AND THE PIN-UP

FRANCE, 1990s

Whisper it quietly, but long-distance cycling can sometimes become a little, you know, tedious. No matter how spectacular the scenery, how fascinating the local fauna and flora or how intriguing the twists and turns of the course, pedalling relentlessly for 100 miles (161km) or more can, frankly, be monotonous. Some riders have been known to listen to audio versions of particularly dull political memoirs just to liven things up a bit.

The daily prolonged grind of the Tour de France is a good example of such potential tedium out on the lonely long and winding road, and faced with mile after mile of identikit French countryside before him, Italian rider Mario Cipollini came up with a rather cheeky antidote.

He was a bit of a lad, Mario, more of which shortly, but for now we are concerned with the visual aids he employed to take his mind off the monotony. More specifically we are focused on the stem of his bike, specially designed in an oval shape to allow our Mario to attach the sticker of his choice to it.

Other less lusty riders might have opted for a map of the course or an inspirational quote or two. Maybe even a picture of the wife and kids. In the 1990s Mario, however, went for a series of images of centrefolds from *Playboy*. It was refreshing of course to find a fella who *didn't* claim to read the magazine for the articles, but Mario's risqué choice caused rather a stir in Tour circles as he rode along brazenly ogling the buxom charms of various scantily clad ladies. His favourite pin-up was none other than the pneumatic Pamela Anderson. Mario couldn't get enough of Pammy, apparently, and as he clocked up the miles, he would gaze adoringly at the sultry star of such cinematic greats as *Barb Wire*, *Scary Movie 3* and the seminal *Blonde and Blonder*.

The raunchy images, however, were only the tip of the iceberg when it came to Mario's rap sheet. The Italian was a one-man publicity-generating machine, and although he never actually finished the Tour – he was a sprinter and could never be bothered with all the huff and puff of the mountain stages – he was rarely out of the headlines.

Nicknamed variously 'Super Mario' and 'Il Re Leone' ('The Lion King'), he forged his reputation as one of cycling's greatest showmen with his outlandish choice of racing uniforms, appearing at the start line at different times in a zebra-pattern suit, a tiger-print outfit and one inspired by the infamous 'Body Worlds' exhibition which displayed his internal organs and muscles. He also wore a techno-themed outfit based on the acclaimed 1982 film *Tron*.

At the 1999 Tour de France he turned up before the start of a day's racing in a chariot dressed as Julius Caesar to celebrate the birthday of Rome's finest, while another day he entertained the crowds when he arranged a stunt in which he was chased by a pride of pantomime lions. Il Re Leone, remember?

Mario once posted a picture of himself on social media completely naked in the saddle (his modesty tactfully preserved) while he was famously photographed puffing on a cigarette *during* a race. His reputation as the bad boy of two wheels was merely cemented when he was caught in a naked tryst with a glamour model on a Sardinian beach by the paparazzi.

So as we said, quite a lad, our Mario. He retired in 2006 and to be fair, when he wasn't courting controversy he did find time to win 12 stages of the Tour de France during his colourful career, and the gold medal in the men's road race at the 2002 UCI World Championships.

STAIRWAY TO HEAVEN

1993

Cyclists have two mortal enemies, terrifying twin threats to their riding pleasure which cast long, dark shadows over all that is good and holy about life on two wheels.

The first is the pernicious puncture, the second the heinous hill. Both are as thoroughly unwelcome as the other, but while that sudden deflating feeling can be remedied with a well-placed patch and a judicious dab of glue, it's simply impossible to ignore a serious slope or irritating incline.

That was until 1993, when the undulating Norwegian city of Trondheim took pity on its poor, exhausted cyclists and installed the world's first bicycle lift. Known as the 'Trampe' (the Norwegian for 'to stomp') the lift was beguilingly easy to use. First you bought a key card to activate the mechanism. Then you got into position, placing your right foot on a metal plate that emerged from a concealed conveyor belt and keeping your left foot on the pedal. All that was left to do was allow the plate to push you and your bike smoothly up the hill, no sweat and no huffing and puffing. Reports of first-time users having a bit of a wobble and tumble were not unheard of but overall the Trampe proved a big hit in Trondheim with locals and tourists alike.

The system was in service for 19 years but in 2012 the city's council decided it was time for an upgrade and the Trampe was replaced by 'CycloCable' – essentially exactly the same but with shinier foot pedals and a new, more expensive logo.

THE CRASH-TEST COPPER

FRANCE, 1994

The police have been bravely employing bikes to thwart the evil machinations of the criminal fraternity since the late 19th century (see 'Bobbies on Bikes', page 169). Two wheels can prove jolly useful when attempting to apprehend fleeing miscreants, and a water-bottle holder is a useful place to store a truncheon.

This particular tale, however, relates to a rather less harmonious hook-up between the long arm of the law and bicycles, and took place at the climax of the first stage of the 1994 Tour de France, which took place between Lille and the small town of Armentières.

The peloton was in full flow as it approached the finish, the riders swinging around the final bend and hitting speeds of up to 37¼mph (60km/h) in the frantic final dash to the line. Belgian Wilfried Nelissen was out of the saddle, head down and pedalling furiously, and might have won had he not ploughed headlong into a policeman who stood in his path.

Our hapless local gendarme was, of course, on hand to police the crowd in Armentières. Metal barriers had been installed to keep the fans at bay, and every 55 yards (50m) or so there was a safety gap in the barrier for the coppers on duty to shelter when the riders flew past. For reasons known only to himself, this particular gendarme had eschewed the sanctuary of his cubby-hole and had unwisely stationed himself on the edge of the course.

Nelissen never saw him coming, and why would he? The gendarme simply shouldn't have been there and the crash that ensued brought down the policeman, the Belgian and four other riders in the peloton with a sickening crunch.

The scene that followed was reminiscent of something from the imagination of Quentin Tarantino. Nelissen and French rider Laurent Jalabert were pictured lying dazed and confused on the road, blood pouring from their numerous injuries before they were rushed to hospital, while the policeman lay on a stretcher with an oxygen mask over his face, his broken leg testament to the full force of the initial collision.

There were suggestions that the gendarme had caused the crash because he was leaning out beyond the barrier to get a photo of the peloton, but an official investigation cleared him and concluded he was merely *un grand imbécile*.

The incident was no laughing matter for Nelissen or Jalabert. The blood-splattered pile-up ended both riders' Tour de France that year and had other far-reaching repercussions. Nelissen was never the same cyclist after the crash, and retired four years later at the age of 28, following another serious collision. Jalabert returned to the ranks after his rehabilitation, but his days as a top-class sprinter were over and he was forced to reinvent himself on the Tour as an all-rounder.

WOMEN, WHEELS
& POLITICS
NORTH KOREA, 1996

It's easy to be critical of Kim Jong-un. The North Korean dictator is, of course, a basket case who has been responsible for ramping up military tensions on the Korean peninsula ever since he got Daddy's job in 2012. He's got a dodgy record on human rights, starves his own people and he keeps threatening to blow the world to kingdom come. Overall, definitely a bit of a despotic nutter then.

But what you probably don't realise is that the chubby tyrant is also a committed champion of women cyclists, and just three months after succeeding the old man Kim Jong-il as supreme leader, he overturned a bizarre 16-year-long ban on the ladies of North Korea getting into the saddle. Which surely means he can't be all bad.

'In perhaps another sign that North Korean society is changing, Chinese media reported that women are being allowed to ride bicycles for the first time for years,' went the NBC website article. 'Cycling for women was banned in 1996 because the activity wasn't regarded as sufficiently feminine by the male-dominated North Korean regime. It is not clear why the female bicycle ban was reversed but it does appear as though the wheels of change in the country are turning.'

So what was Kim's motivation? Chasing the female vote seems unlikely because North Koreans already do exactly as they're told at election time or face the consequences.

Maybe he'd just bought shares in the state bicycle company or he was trying to prove he was in touch with his feminine side. Perhaps he was planning a new female bicycle regiment to wage war against the Western oppressors. The truth is, we just don't know.

Sadly North Korea is not alone in discouraging female cyclists, and in 2012 the debate in Iran about the morality of women on wheels was reignited when the ultra-conservative Ayatollah Elm Alhuda raged against the dangers of pedal-powered sexual equality.

'It is not a sin for a woman to sit on a bicycle saddle, provided she does so indoors or in her backyard,' he said from sometime in the Dark Ages. 'But if she cycles in public her movements and posture will lead to corruption and prostitution.'

Exactly where Alhuda stands on the thorny issue of spin classes is unclear.

TWO WHEELS
VERSUS FOUR LEGS

FRANCE, 1997

There's a saying about closing the stable doors after the horse has bolted, and never has the old adage been more apt or more comical than back in 1997, when an errant steed made an impromptu appearance during the Criterium International race in France, an equine invasion that was thankfully captured by television cameras.

The race was wending its merry way on rural roads near Toulouse when the peloton found itself riding parallel to a field. In said field was our horse who, on spying the riders, began enthusiastically galloping alongside them.

The 'shadow' racing was short-lived, though, as the horse quickly came to the end of its paddock, but rather than call it a day, it leapt a gate and joined the stunned riders on the road. The majority of the peloton fanned out to avoid the unregistered racer, but seven competitors were initially unable to pull safely over and for a few hundred metres were forced to look nervously over their shoulders as the four-legged interloper breathed down their necks.

The horse then sprinted to the head of the peloton and overtook the motorbike at the front of the race, inadvertently becoming an unlikely equine pacesetter. It could have won, too, but just 11¾ miles (19km) from the finish it finally realised its faux pas and stopped for a bit of a graze.

The live commentary of the incident was almost as hilarious as the images. When the horse began running in the field, the commentators initially found the sight rather endearing, but when it vaulted the gate and scattered the riders, they became animated and someone in the studio actually uttered the immortal words 'Ooh la la!' That is absolutely true.

If you're a fan of French cinema all this may sound vaguely familiar, as the footage of our friend gate-crashing the Criterium was briefly featured in 2001 romantic comedy *Amélie*, perhaps the greatest equine performance in the movies since *The Godfather*.

AN UNLIKELY
MEDICAL HERO

ENGLAND, 2000

It was not so many pages ago that we learned all about the birth of BMX in America in the early 1970s (see 'BMX Gets a "BUM" Deal', page 100), and not long after the craze had gripped the States, it found its way across the Atlantic and a new generation of British kids were suddenly bunny hopping, bar spinning and tail whipping.

One of our leading BMXers back then was a young fella called Tom Lynch, who travelled the world with his bike in the 1980s and won countless individual and team titles. He was seriously good, our Tom.

In 1992 however he decided to get a 'proper' job and joined the London Ambulance Service as a paramedic. He didn't know it then but it was a career move that would eventually revolutionise emergency medical care in the capital and beyond.

Tom quickly got fed up with the notoriously sedate pace of London traffic. His ambulance's flashing blue light was all well and good but Tom, of course, was thinking of a way of getting to his patients as quickly as possible on two rather than four wheels.

'All the time I was thinking how much faster I could get around on my bike,' he explained sensibly. 'But every time I said this to my colleagues, or bosses, they thought I was joking. Eventually I had spoken about it for so long that in 2000 I was allowed to set up a trial run. I knew it would work, all I needed to do was ride a bike fast and do my job when I got there.'

The London Ambulance Cycle Response unit was born and today there are 12 teams working in the capital across the city's 69 ambulance stations. The paramedics ride specially modified Rockhopper bikes and carry 59½lb (27kg) of potentially life-saving gear. They cover an average of 24⅘ miles (40km) per shift and have saved an estimated £300,000 per year on fuel bills. In its first decade of operation Cycle Response paramedics treated 50,000 people, freeing up 5,000 ambulance hours annually.

'Seven or eight times out of ten, we're arriving on the scene before ambulances purely because we can cut through the traffic,' Lynch said. 'This means that, in about 40 per cent of all cases, we can actually call off the ambulance if the injuries are minor enough, which frees up crews to attend more serious incidents.'

'To be honest, if I have a successful cardiac arrest outcome or hear that someone who I have trained has saved the life of someone who is now walking around healthy, it's the best thing in the world. It's like winning a gold medal every time.'

Cities like Norwich, Cambridge, Leeds, Liverpool and Manchester followed London's lead, as well as cities across the world, and in 2007 Tom's pioneering efforts were recognised when he was awarded an MBE.

Hopefully you were blissfully unaware of the history of two-wheeled triage before reading this, but should you ever be grateful for the prompt response of a paramedic on a bike, you now know who to thank.

LAURA'S LEARNING CURVE
ENGLAND, 2000

The origins of the famous proverb, 'If at first you don't succeed, try, try, try again' are debatable. The 19th-century educational writer W.E. Hickson is credited with popularising the saying, but it apparently first appeared in print in a 1848 novel entitled *The Children of the New Forest* by Captain Frederick Marryat.

We can now leave Hickson and Marryat to bicker posthumously over bragging rights, because what concerns us here is the essence of the maxim, the exhortation never to wave the white flag when things do not initially go according to plan. It is, in the immortal if unwieldy words of footballer Iain Dowie, all about bouncebackability.

Many have prospered in the face of early adversity. J.K. Rowling's first *Harry Potter* book was rejected by publishers 12 times before Bloomsbury decided her tale of prepubescent wizards and witches might be worth a punt, while Bill Gates' first business venture went bust before he found the Midas touch with Microsoft.

In the world of cycling the inimitable Laura Trott is the embodiment of pluck. The diminutive four-time Olympic gold medallist was born prematurely with a collapsed lung and subsequently diagnosed with asthma, but that didn't stop her sweeping all before her in the velodrome.

It is though her early, unedifying experiences in the saddle that reveal her true grit. The future champion got her first set of wheels back in 2000, and her first experience in the saddle did little to suggest the girl from Hertfordshire would become a global star.

'My first cycling memory is from when my parents bought me a road bike but I was too small for it,' she said. 'The handlebars were too far away and I couldn't pull the brakes. I crashed into a barrier, which my dad wasn't impressed with. I also crashed at [the outdoor velodrome at Welwyn Garden City] because my dad didn't screw my pedal in properly and it fell off. I was only eight – I didn't know how to use an Allen key.'

Lesser characters might have thrown in the towel but Laura was obviously made of sterner stuff, and she was back on the Welwyn track later the same year to win a 500m event, her first ever race victory which came with a princely purse of £2 for the first over the line.

The rest is ongoing history. Laura was only 24 when she won gold in the Team Pursuit and Omnium at the Olympic Games in Rio de Janeiro in 2016 to take her Games tally to four and make her Great Britain's most successful ever female Olympian. Falling off her bike remains an occupational hazard, but thankfully it was one that didn't deter her in the embryonic stages of her remarkable career.

SIR BRADLEY'S VEGETARIAN PORKIES

ENGLAND, 2001

Vegetarianism isn't for everyone. Some people just can't survive on nut cutlets and Quorn alone, and for them the allure of the steak and the sausage is simply irresistible. If God hadn't meant us to embrace our inner carnivore, they argue, why did he make certain animals so bloody tasty?

The meat eaters and the veggies rarely see eye to eye, and the divide between the two camps presented Sir Bradley Wiggins with an interesting dilemma back in 2001 when he was forced to choose between honesty and the chance to race professionally for the first time.

Wiggo's quandary came when he was invited to ride for the Linda McCartney Racing Team. Set up by Linda and Beatles hubby Paul three years earlier, they'd made history when they became the first British team to enter the prestigious Giro d'Italia and there were big plans to compete at the Tour de France and the UCI World Cup.

The problem was all the team's riders had to be vegetarian. There were to be no exceptions, and with Wiggins partial to a Sunday roast and the odd burger, he didn't exactly meet the team's strict criteria. His solution of course was to be as economical as possible with the truth.

'The worst thing about being in the Linda McCartney team was pretending to be a vegetarian,' he admitted in an interview with the *Daily Mail* years later. 'I think everyone was sneaking in the bacon sandwiches.'

Fortunately Wiggins did not have to maintain his dietary deception for long and before he even had the chance to race, the team was suddenly disbanded with reported debts of nearly £1 million and a dispute with the Union Cycliste Internationale over unpaid riders' wages.

'The whole experience was a disaster, basically a lesson in how not to run a team,' he said. 'It was completely disorganised, the funding wasn't there and you had to be a vegetarian. Instinctively, I ran for home, which in cycling terms meant Team GB, who were fantastic and secured me the Category A Lottery funding again. They could not have been more supportive and they helped ensure that a drama didn't become a crisis.'

It was certainly money well spent as Wiggins famously went on to win the Tour de France in 2012 as well as his fourth Olympic gold medal at the London Games later in the year. He remains a committed carnivore.

MANSER'S AFRICAN ODYSSEY

AFRICA, 2003

Africa is a big continent. Really enormous when you think that, were you to circumnavigate the entire length of the African coastline, you would clock up a staggering 22,991 miles (37,000km).

That's a hell of a lot of pedalling if you were to undertake the epic journey on a humble bicycle, but such trifling obstacles did not deter South African adventurer Riaan Manser when he decided to accept exactly that daunting challenge, an ambitious expedition that very nearly killed him.

Manser set off on his trusty mountain bike from Cape Town in September 2003. He averaged an impressive 55 miles (88.5km) per day and after two years, two months and 15 days in the saddle, travelling through 34 different countries, he had become the first person to circumnavigate Africa on two wheels.

His trek was not without incident. He had to overcome both the heat and humidity of the Sahara and the Libyan deserts, was forced to eat monkey, rat and bat to sustain himself en route, and was thrown into jail in Equatorial Guinea after refusing to pay a bribe to border police. He was twice stopped and questioned by Al Qaeda in Algeria, but it was in Liberia where Manser's journey nearly came to a premature and grisly conclusion.

'Our foreign affairs department said they'd withdraw all diplomatic support if I were to enter Liberian territory,' he explained.

'I got into Liberia and I could just sense things were wrong. I walked through a village that had just been burnt out. There were children's toys and suitcases torn open, people's houses and lives destroyed.

'The next day I was pulled off my bicycle in the jungle by guys so high on drugs they were falling around. Then they beat me, 13-year-olds were literally beating me up. Four or five hours later, when they had me in a holding cell, about five or six of them were saying to each other, "Let's gut him, let's kill him, we're wasting time". I'm a brave guy but my knees were shaking. I realised that that day, 26 February 2004, was the day I was going to die.

'Luckily, I had a magazine with me with our former president Thabo Mbeki's picture in it. One guy recognised the photo and said it was his friend ... and he started laughing. I started laughing with him and 20 minutes later he just said to me out of the blue, "Now go before we kill you." I climbed on my bicycle and got out of there.'

Manser's feat was recognised when he was named 'Adventurer of the Year' by *Out There* magazine in 2006 and granted an audience with Nelson Mandela. He politely declined an offer to work for the Liberian Tourist Board.

HORSES FOR COURSES

FRANCE, 2003

As befits cycling's most famous and popular race, and one that now boasts more than a century of history, the Tour de France has many fascinating and quirky traditions. Examples include the presentation of a toy lion and bunch of flowers to the winner, the wearing of iconic coloured jerseys by the leading rider, sprinter and mountain climber as the race unfolds and the expectation that the eventual champion will share his winner's cheque with his teammates.

It is though not only the race itself that basks in its history, and in the more rural part of France fans of the Tour have their own way of celebrating the annual race, jumping as they do into their own saddles and riding horses on adjacent tracks and nearby fields in parallel with the peloton. It certainly makes for great TV when the cameras capture the locals galloping along on a steed at the same pace as Chris Froome.

The tradition was proudly maintained during the 2003 Tour, but sadly for the jockeys in question the cameras were on hand to record their embarrassing moment of equine misfortune.

The first horse-related mishap took place in a field alongside the course. Three young riders had saddled up to canter along with the cyclists, and all seemed to be going swimmingly until one horse veered suddenly to the left and caused another to rear, throwing its jockey off in a crumpled heap. All, of course, was caught on camera for the evening TV news.

And that wasn't even the most spectacular equine misadventure of the stage. Later in the day the news crews following the race spied a young child in another field on a tiny pony, the diminutive steed's little legs going like the clappers in a valiant attempt to keep up with the peloton. Unfortunately the pony's impressive pace was too much for the child, who fell off. The real indignity, however, followed as the kid fell in front of the pony, which caused the petite steed to do a spectacular somersault over its erstwhile junior jockey. Both incidents can be viewed in all their inglorious detail via the Internet.

And if you are about to boot up your PC or open your laptop, and since we're ploughing an equine furrow here, you might want to take a look at a bizarre black-and-white photo taken during the 1975 Tour, which documents the moment a riderless white horse decided to join the two-wheeled fray.

For the record, both unfortunate riders in 2003, not to mention their horses, suffered no serious injuries after their tumbles so it's OK to laugh. Or not. You can please yourself.

THE NUMBERS GAME
SOUTH AFRICA, 2004

A grand total of 219 competitors assembled on the starting line for the Tour de France in 2013, but if you think that's a lot of riders, you've never witnessed the spectacular sight of South Africa's record-breaking Cape Argus Pick 'n' Pay Cycle Tour in full flow.

The 'Argus', as it's known to its friends, regularly attracts over 35,000 professional and amateur cyclists alike and proudly holds the record for the world's largest individually timed race, when an incredible 42,614 saddled up and set off on the 67¾-mile (109km) circular course back in 2004.

The brainchild of friends Bill Mylrea and John Stegmann, the Argus was originally organised as a way to highlight the need for more cycle paths in South Africa, and a modest 525 riders turned up for the first race in 1978, pedalling their way from Cape Town down the Cape Peninsula and back into the city.

Numbers grew steadily over the years, and in 1989 the Argus broke through the five-figure barrier for the first time. Six years later they had more 20,000 entrants and by the end of the century there were over 30,000 riders.

The record-breaking year of 2004 saw 42,614 start the race in March and 31,219 complete the course. Italian Antonio Salamone won the men's race in a time of two hours, 32 minutes and 23 seconds while South African Anke Erlank was the fastest woman on the day.

The milestone was officially recognised by Guinness World Records, and after the Argus organisers decided to cap the number of entrants at 35,000 in 2011, it's a record that could stand uncontested for years to come.

MUDDYING THE WATERS

WALES, 2005

Mountain bikes are designed for rough terrain. Going off-road is their raison d'être, and any self-respecting mountain bike will positively relish the chance to abandon the namby-pamby tarmac of a pristine highway and get its tyres dirty in the great outdoors.

But even the most testosterone-fuelled bicycle baulks when it hears the dreaded words 'World Mountain Bike Bog Snorkelling Championship', the annual gathering in Wales in which bikes are pushed to their absolute limit. And then a bit more.

First staged in 2005 at the Waen Rhydd Bog near Llanwrtyd, the 'WMBBSC' (as we shall call it for the sake of brevity) is a fiendish test of man and machine and requires a very specific set of modifications before riders are allowed to compete to set the fastest time over two lengths of a 40 yards (36.6m), 6ft (1.8m) deep water-filled trench cut through the peat.

Firstly, the air in the bike's tyres has to be replaced with water and the bicycle weighed down by lead weights to avoid competitors experiencing unfair buoyancy. Secondly, and for the same reason, the riders themselves must wear a weighted rucksack. Thirdly, they must also don a snorkel and diving mask to guard against drowning (and because it looks hilarious).

And then they're off. It's tough work for the competitors as they try to power through the mud and silt, and it's not much fun for the bikes either as they spend the entire race submerged under the filthy water.

'It's very murky, you can't see much in the bog and it doesn't taste too good either,' said 40-year-old Bryan Evans from Bridgend after he won the men's competition in a record time of one minute and one second in 2007. 'I'm really relieved that it is over more than anything. You can't really train for this type of event and there is a big element of luck involved because you can go into a pothole and fall over. It's a bit of fun more than anything.'

The true bicycling masochist, however, can go one stage even further and enter the infamous Bog Triathlon at Llanwrtyd which begins with a 12-mile (19.3km) run, two lengths swimming in the peat bog before climaxing with a 24⅘-mile (40km) mountain cycle. Which all sounds like even more, if not exactly clean, 'fun'.

THE FOLD-AWAY PHENOMENON

SPAIN, 2006

The first Brompton bike rolled off the production line in London in 1981. The company initially built just 30 of their iconic fold-up cycles, but the concept proved hugely popular and today they manufacture over 22,000 bicycles a year, exporting them to more than 40 countries.

They're definitely a design classic, and if you don't fancy lugging an unwieldy mountain bike onto a packed commuter train, or trying to stuff your 20-speed racer into the boot of your car, the Brompton is the bike for you.

The only drawback is they're not built for speed. Their 16-inch wheels are never going to enable riders to break the land speed record, and practicality rather than alacrity are the watchwords of the company.

But that didn't stop one bright spark coming up with the idea of the Brompton World Championship in 2006, a unique race that sees Brompton enthusiasts from across the world congregating for an annual test of pedal power.

The unusual race was first staged in Barcelona in 2006. Two years later it moved to Blenheim Palace in Oxfordshire, England, and after a stint as part of the Orbital Cycling Festival at the Goodwood motor circuit, the final of the world's largest gathering of fold-up bikes was held in London in 2016, following qualifying events in 13 different countries with competitors starting on The Mall before completing eight laps of St James's Park.

The rules of the race are simple and endearingly quirky. All competitors must wear a jacket and tie – absolutely no Lycra allowed – and the start sees competitors sprint from a staging area to their bikes, which they must unfold as quickly as possible. It's then on with the serious business of racing over the 9.6-mile (15.5km) course.

The 2012 event attracted over 800 registrants from 34 countries. As well as prizes for the fastest male and female riders, there are also awards for the best-dressed competitors, and the event has proved so popular that spin-off national championships have sprung up as far afield as Korea, Japan and the USA.

Although it's billed as a fun day out, the event also attracts a smattering of professional riders and in 2012 it was Michael Hutchinson, the reigning national champion over 50 miles (80.5km), who was the men's winner with a record time of 20 minutes and 17 seconds.

'It's pretty different,' Hutchinson admitted. 'Most events are a bit more formal but normally a lot smaller in terms of rider numbers. There's a much greater variety of riders. Some competitors are there for a different kind of a day out, some are deadly serious and there are any number of different approaches in between. It is quite a lot more fun than most events.'

WHO LET THE DOGS OUT?

FRANCE, 2007

They say a dog is a man's best friend but riders in the Tour de France would disagree vehemently, vulnerable as they are to sudden and unexpected canine incursions onto the route of the race and the carnage that inevitably follows.

One of the most recent examples of a dog-induced crash came in 2007, when Sandy Casar was minding his own business in a breakaway group on the 18th stage of the race when a black Labrador casually emerged from a knot of spectators by the side of the road and cleaned the Frenchman out. Casar inadvertently took down Belgium's Frederick Willems in the process and the pair scraped to a painful halt.

Casar, however, was nothing if not, ahem, dogged. He picked himself up and despite blood dripping from his right buttock, he amazingly still managed to win the stage. The offending dog couldn't understand what all the fuss was about.

A few days earlier, it had been the turn of German Marcus Burghardt to curse the intervention of one of our four-legged 'friends'. Burghardt was part of the peloton during the ninth stage of the Tour when a Golden Retriever ambled innocently in front of him, sending the German rider flying over his handlebars. The portly pooch had obviously been overdoing it on the Pedigree Chum because the impact of the collision buckled Burghardt's front wheel.

Five years later Philippe Gilbert became the latest victim of a canine collision as he rode on the 18th stage from Blagnac to Brive-la-Gaillarde. Once again the dog, an enormous black mongrel, wandered onto the course like he owned the place and the Belgian, plus seven other competitors, hit the tarmac.

Gilbert was steaming. He dusted himself off and marched over to the family who had allowed their pampered pooch to stray and gave them a piece of his mind. They responded by cowering silently behind their young daughter.

To add insult to injury, the rider was almost run over by a support vehicle as he turned to rejoin the race. 'His hand has been injured a little as well as his elbow and knee,' said BMC team manager John Lelangue at the end of the day. 'The dog was stronger than him and it won that bout but the important thing is that he could return to his place in the peloton.'

The dog was unavailable for comment.

THE LOVE THAT DARE NOT SPEAK ITS NAME

SCOTLAND, 2007

We all adore our bicycles but it's very important to draw a clear line between affection and infatuation. Letting our feelings for our two-wheeled friends run wild can only end in tears and, in this extreme example, a three-year probationary prison sentence.

Readers of a sensitive disposition are advised to avert their eyes now.

The bizarre bicycle case occurred in Scotland in 2007 when a 51-year-old man called Robert Stewart failed to open his door when cleaners turned up to tidy his room at a hostel in Ayr. Unfortunately for our man, the cleaners had a job to do and weren't taking no for an answer.

'They knocked on the door several times and there was no reply,' prosecutor Gail Davidson told Ayr Sheriff Court at Stewart's rather embarrassing trial. 'They used a master key to unlock the door and they then observed the accused wearing only a white T-shirt, naked from the waist down. The accused was holding the bike and moving his hips back and forth as if to simulate sex.'

Stewart initially claimed it was all a misunderstanding, but he knew he was bang to rights and eventually admitted a sexually aggravated breach of the peace by conducting himself in a disorderly manner and simulating sex.

'In almost four decades in the law I thought I had come across every perversion known to mankind,' admitted shocked Sheriff Colin Miller. 'This is a new one on me. I have never heard of a "cycle-sexualist".' Quite, but it seems that bawdy behaviour with bikes is more widespread than we feared and in 2013 there was another incident of two-wheeled titillation.

It happened in the Östersund area of Sweden and came to light after bike owner Per Edstrom grew tired of finding his tyres punctured on an almost daily basis. He set up a covert camera to shed light on what the hell was going on but perhaps wished he hadn't when he was confronted with graphic images of a man approaching the bicycle, puncturing the wheels and then, ahem, 'enjoying' himself. Manually.

'I am not scared of him, just irritated over all the punctures I have had to fix,' said Edstrom after the shocking discovery. 'This man is probably completely harmless, bicycles are just his thing.'

YOU'VE BEEN FRAMED
USA, 2007

There's nothing in the cycling rule book that says the frame has to be made of metal. Alloys of iron, aluminium, titanium and even magnesium are all jolly good materials, and while thermoplastics and carbon fibres have tried to muscle in on the metal monopoly in recent years, there are more green solutions.

In 2007, for example, a company called Daedalus Custom Bamboo Bikes unveiled a novel new bicycle constructed from, well, bamboo, obviously. It wasn't cheap at over £800 per bike but joint creators Liakos Ariston and Jacob Prinz insisted it had a strength-to-weight ratio to rival some types of steel and that the flexibility of the bamboo offered a remarkably smooth ride.

'We've gained a lot more respect for the material we work with,' said Ariston at the big launch. 'We've had a few accidents on them and generally riders and bikes have come out unscathed.'

The pair drew inspiration from bamboo woodworkers in Thailand but the manufacturing process was not exactly rapid. In fact, the enterprising duo had to let their carefully selected lengths of bamboo 'relax' in their workshop for 18 months before they were ready to be fashioned into a frame, meaning you really had to get your order in early.

Four years after the bamboo bike was unleashed on an unsuspecting world, a Chinese man unveiled a fully functioning cycle crafted almost entirely from lollipop sticks. Only the chain of 35-year-old Sun Chao's creation was not made from sticks, and although the ride on the wooden wheels wasn't exactly comfortable, his bizarre creation definitely worked.

Chao got the lollipop-building bug after watching a man on television make a model ship for his girlfriend – the man's girlfriend, not our Chao's. He started making his own small-scale models before working up to his magnum opus, the bike. It took 10,000 sticks to make his grand design a reality, although he had the sense to bulk order them rather than licking his way to his required total.

PLUMBING NEW DEPTHS
ITALY, 2008

We have already heard about the feat of astronaut Alan Bean and his gravity-free pedalling (see 'Out of This World', page 98) but space is only one of cycling's brave new worlds, and in 2008 Vittorio Innocente decided to head in completely the opposite direction, setting a new world record for the deepest underwater bike ride.

The 62-year-old Italian set his bizarre milestone in the waters of Portofino's maritime marine reserve in the Mediterranean, on a specially adapted cycle with the tyres filled with water rather than air and 77lb (35kg) of ballast, to prove once again there's nothing someone with far too much time on their hands cannot achieve.

Innocente was lowered into the water by a bemused team of local scuba divers. At a depth of 91⅘ ft (28m) he mounted his trusty bike, and after nine minutes of submerged pedalling following the route of a natural underwater slope, he had managed to ride down to a depth of 213⅓ ft (65m).

In case you're wondering, Innocente *was* equipped with the necessary scuba gear. He's mad, not insane.

'I had to click up a gear to make pedalling easier,' he said once he was safely back on terra firma and the record had been confirmed by Guinness World Records. 'It was tough because I ran into more mud than I expected.'

Four years after Innocente's challenge, more underwater cycling was attempted when former Royal Marines Chris

Sirett and Brian Stokes suddenly decided they had an irresistible urge to set a new record for the longest distance pedalled sub aqua on a static bike.

They chose the 2012 Southampton Boat Show for their attempt, setting up an exercise bike in a giant, glass-fronted tank and, taking it in turns, got down to business.

Their original target was to clock up 250 miles (402km) in 24 hours, but things didn't go quite according to plan and after 15 hours in the tank, they were hauled out after beginning to feel unwell. They did however set the record, with a total distance of 100⅛ miles (161km) covered.

The record for the furthest solo distance cycled in H_2O meanwhile belongs to Germany's Jens Stotzner, who managed to clock up 6,708m (7,340 yards) around the bottom of a swimming pool in his homeland in 2013. That's 78 laps of the pool and presumably took place after 'Aqua Aerobics for the Elderly' had finished.

For those of you interested in joining the underwater cycling fraternity, it's worth remembering that bikes do tend to rust rather rapidly when submerged.

THE MADNESS OF
SIR DAVE

ENGLAND, 2008

Dave Brailsford possesses what you might politely describe as an acute eye for detail. Less charitably, you'd have to say the long-serving performance director of British Cycling has an incurable compulsive disorder, but the ends justify the means, and since his appointment in 2002, he has overseen the emergence of the most successful two-wheeled team in the nation's history.

Sir Dave, as we will temporarily refer to him, is notorious for his meticulousness, and from ensuring his riders have the right pillows in their hotel bedrooms to guarantee a revitalising night's sleep to washing their hands correctly to avoid infection and potential illness, the Ubermeister of British cycling has left no stone unturned in his pursuit of success and medals.

He even ordered every single race suit worn by British riders at the Beijing Olympics in 2008 to be shredded in case any rival nations should get their dirty mitts on them and decode the secrets of the material that many believed had played a major role in the team's triumphs.

Team GB's performance in Athens, the Beijing Games four years later and their wonderful performance at London 2012 – amassing a grand total of 18 gold medals in the process – suggests dear old Dave's methods have been nothing but positive in outcome, but even he admits he's occasionally trodden a fine line between obsession and utter lunacy.

His potential moment of madness came in the build-up to the Beijing Games. Big Dave was pondering the perennial problem of the broken collarbone – the most common injury in cycling – and hit on an innovative (but, of course, secret) form of treatment to get the rider back in the saddle as quickly as possible. All he needed was a willing but appropriately injured guinea pig.

'Ed Clancy [who went on to win gold in the team pursuit] said he would not mind having his two collarbones broken,' Brailsford admitted in an interview in 2009. 'But then, thankfully, someone said "what on earth are you doing?" and this madness was stopped.'

Thank heavens for that. Quite why Clancy was so eager for a trip to the fracture clinic is a mystery but the fact that Brailsford seriously entertained the idea is the real worry. His theories on how best to treat saddle sores really don't bear thinking about.

AIN'T NO SUNSHINE
ANY MORE
ENGLAND, 2008

Ever since the dawn of time, Man has sought to harness the enormous power of the sun. Swiss scientist Horace-Bénédict de Saussure (crazy name, crazy guy) really got the ball rolling in 1767 when he created the first solar collector – an insulated box covered with three layers of glass – and since then, great strides have been made in converting sunshine into something really useful.

William J. Bailey (sensible name, sensible guy) moved things on with his 'Copper Collector' in 1908, and in 1970 big business moved in when Exxon (stupid name, dubious environmental record) manufactured the first affordable solar panels. By the time the first prototype solar car was tested in Australia, it looked like we'd cracked it.

Cycling dejectedly lagged behind for years when it came to the sunshine free-for-all, but that all looked set to change in 2008 when a London-based design company proudly unveiled their bright yellow 'Cycle Sol', promising it would revolutionise the lives of two-wheeled commuters.

'It is just like an electric bike but the motor runs on a battery that is powered by solar energy,' explained Miroslav Miljevic (tricky name, clever guy), the boffin behind the concept.

'There is a large flexible panel on the roof which is covered in solar cells that soak up the sun. You can leave it outside the office during the day to top up the rechargable [battery] ready for the ride home.

'These days solar cells are pretty good at picking up the lowest amount of light so it should still work when the skies are cloudy. At night time the small battery can be charged using the mains electricity in just a few hours. I believe it is just what the modern-day commuter needs; it helps you along your way while also being kind to the environment. And if the worst happens and it rains, the roof will keep you dry.'

You've probably seen hundreds, nay thousands of Cycle Sols on the streets of London and other major cities across the country. No? A fundamental design flaw, you say?

Britain, of course, isn't exactly blessed with lashings of sunshine. There's sometimes a couple of weeks in July that aren't absolutely awful, but sun-drenched we are not, which probably explains why the Cycle Sol hasn't exactly been a big hit. Time, perhaps, for Miroslav to get back to his drawing board.

GOING FOR GOLD

SWEDEN, 2008

If you're familiar with the TV show *Pimp My Ride*, you'll already be aware that there's no shortage of people with a penchant for customising their cars. The results are invariably a psychedelic nightmare of colour framed with ridiculously big wheels, but it makes the owners happy and their probation officers don't seem to mind.

Bicycles, of course, are not immune to a spot of pimping either (see 'Chicago Defies Convention', page 76), but a Swedish company perhaps got too carried away in 2008 when it built 10 bikes with frames made out of 24-carat gold. Costing an eye-watering £70,000 each, the bicycles were also covered in over 600 Swarovski crystals, but if you're worried they were a tad overpriced, they did come with a leather saddle, a ten-year guarantee and the promise of free delivery to any address in the world. So you'd save a bit of the postage and packaging at least.

The gold bikes, however, were positively low-rent compared to the two-wheeled offering from artist Damien Hirst, a controversial bicycle that eventually sold at auction for a staggering £325,000.

Hirst had already gained notoriety after pickling a cow, a tiger shark and a sheep in formaldehyde all in the name of art, and he continued his one-man assault on the animal kingdom with his bicycle adaptation, taking a Trek Madone model and lacquering the frame with real butterfly wings.

'This is barbaric and horrific,' fumed Sam Glover of People for the Ethical Treatment of Animals. 'Damien Hirst is a one-trick pony. Butterflies are beautiful creatures who should be enjoyed in the wild, not encased in a bike.'

Unsurprisingly Hirst was unrepentant at the time. 'The technical problems were immense as I wanted to use real butterflies and not just pictures of butterflies,' he said. 'I wanted it to shimmer when the light catches it like only real butterflies do, and we were trying not to add any extra weight to the bike.'

The bike went for a record £325,000 at Sotheby's in New York in 2012 but it's probably safe to assume its value dropped dramatically a few months later.

The bike, you see, was specially designed by Hirst for that Lance Armstrong chap. The disgraced American rider pedalled it during the final stage of the 2009 Tour de France but since he was exposed as cycling's greatest cheat, Armstrong's reputation has nosedived. The bike's value has probably followed a similar trajectory.

COPENHAGEN'S CONGESTED CLAIM TO FAME

DENMARK, 2008

Nirvana for the urban cyclist is a city bereft of beastly cars. It remains more dream than reality for the world's millions of metropolitan riders but as fans of *South Pacific* will be acutely aware, 'if you don't have a dream, how you going to have a dream come true?'

Many places have taken great strides to redress the balance between the internal combustion engine and pedal power but perhaps none more so than Copenhagen, a city that proudly lays claim to the busiest cycling street in the world.

According to local government statistics, 36 per cent of the city's 562,000 residents commute to work by bike every day and an estimated 38,000 of them travel along the 'Noerrebrogade' thoroughfare (that's North Bridge Street for those not fluent in Danish), making it the world's most tyre-treaded urban avenue.

The transformation of Copenhagen into a cycling paradise began in 2008 when the city council closed off the Noerrebrogade to cars for a three-month trial. It all went splendidly despite protests from a few local shopkeepers, and at the end of the year they announced the evil car would be banished forever.

The deluge of new cyclists did, however, present the city with problems, and in 2009 they had to introduce a second lane on the Noerrebrogade to accommodate the quicker riders and defuse growing tensions with the more leisurely commuters who now pedal sedately on the inside lane.

A year later, the street had become so popular with cyclists that congestion was becoming a real concern. 'Copenhagen's roads are overloaded with people who want to ride their bicycles in all kinds of weather,' admitted Danish Cyclist Federation spokesman Frits Bredal. 'It's a mode of transportation used by all social classes – even politicians ride bikes.'

The revelation that pesky politicians were taking to two wheels briefly helped to keep numbers down, but the council was forced to announce plans for 'superhighways' for the city's cyclists, accelerating the process of change, and there are now 621 miles (1,000km) of bicycle lanes in and around the Copenhagen area.

Car drivers are now firmly in the minority in the Danish capital, a reversal in commuting fortunes which other cities across the world have been watching with interest.

RISING TO THE OCCASION
ITALY, 2008

Doping has sadly scarred the image of professional cycling over the decades, but the surprise discovery of a rather unusual haul of drugs during the 2008 Giro d'Italia was the cause for a lot of schoolboy sniggering rather than criminal proceedings and recrimination.

The bizarre story unfolded something like this: a car carrying Natalino Moletta, the father of Italian rider Andrea, from Padua to join up with the race was pulled over by the Old Bill and after a thorough search, they found 82 packets of Viagra, a syringe hidden inside a tube of toothpaste and a portable fridge containing a mysterious fluid.

It initially didn't look good for the Moletta family until someone pointed out that Viagra wasn't actually a banned substance and no laws had technically been broken. Moletta Senior was bailed and the long arm of the law sent off the unidentified liquid for testing.

It transpired it was 'Lutelef', which in tiny amounts can be used as an alternative to Viagra.

The suspicion, of course, was that some cyclists were beginning to use Viagra in some way to boost performance, but then some bright spark pointed out a rider was unlikely to use a drug with well-documented 'boosting' qualities while wearing tight Lycra shorts in the full glare of the cameras and thousands of eagle-eyed spectators.

It was a mystery all right. Unsurprisingly, no one came forward to claim ownership of the famed blue pills, and although Moletta was initially suspended by his Gerolsteiner team and pulled out of the Giro, neither he nor his dad were ever charged. Moletta Senior always maintained there was no dodgy plan for the cargo but, equally, never did offer an explanation for why he was in possession of so much Viagra. Mrs Moletta also refused to comment.

THE SUMMIT OF CYCLING
CHINA, 2009

We have already discussed how cyclists and hills are not natural bosom buddies (see 'Stairway to Heaven', page 126), but while most amateurs curse the sight of a energy-sapping gradient, some riders actively seek out the big climbs all in the name of adventure.

Two such intrepid souls were Germans Gil Bretschneider and Peer Schepanski, who decided to take on Mount Muztagata in the Xinjiang Province of China in 2009 on two wheels, a fearsome 24,757ft (7,546m) slope, which is perpetually clad in snow and ice.

The first recorded attempt to climb Muztagata, which translates as 'father of ice mountains', was made by Swedish explorer Sven Hedin back in 1894, but he failed to reach the summit and it was not until 1956 that a team of Chinese and Russian mountaineers finally made it to the top.

Unperturbed, Bretschneider and Schepanski set off on their specially modified bikes with extra-wide tyres to combat the treacherous icy conditions on 23 June, leaving their base camp which sat at an altitude of 17,553ft (5,350m). By 10 July, they had slogged their way to a height of 23,658ft (7,211m) and although they could not quite make it all the way up Muztagata, it was still a new milestone for the highest ever bike ride.

A Latvian chap by the name of Bruno Sulcs did reach the peak of the mountain with his bike at his first attempt, but pictures of his earlier ascent reveal he carried his bicycle on his back rather than pedalling his way up, only getting into the saddle for his rather hair-raising descent. Which was, frankly, missing the point entirely.

In 1996, the late Swedish adventurer Göran Kropp launched a bold attempt to scale Everest without bottled oxygen or the help of Sherpas, and while he was wasn't stupid enough to try to cycle up the world's tallest mountain, he did warm up for the considerable challenge by riding the 8,000 miles (12,875km) from Sweden to base camp.

Kropp set off from Stockholm on 16 October 1995 on his modified mount, carrying 238lb (108kg) of equipment and food, and finally reached the Himalayas in April 1996.

The Swede got to within 984ft (300m) of the summit on his first attempt before he was forced to turn back. He had to wait three more weeks before he finally stood on top of the world and Kropp celebrated by promptly jumping back into the saddle and cycling part of the way home. Mad doesn't even come close, does it?

BOBBIES ON BIKES

UK, 2009

The sight of a police officer on patrol on his bicycle is a common one. Our boys and girls in blue have long since used two wheels to get the job done and many a criminal has been apprehended thanks to pedal power.

One of the first forces to turn to bikes in the ongoing war against wrongdoers was the Kent Constabulary, who purchased 20 bicycles at a cost of £8 each back in 1896. Just eight years later, they had 129 two-wheel rural patrols operating in the county, and the popularity of cycles as an intrinsic part of the bobby's kit, like the truncheon and fabled notebook, quickly spread. Today, London's Metropolitan Police have some 2,500 bicycles at their disposal to keep the streets of the capital free from crime.

There was, however, a bit of a hoo-ha in 2009 about the Old Bill's wheel-mounted divisions when it emerged that perhaps not all their officers were quite as proficient in the saddle as they should be.

The almighty row erupted when the Association of Chief Police Officers (ACPO) announced their intention to publish a 93-page pamphlet entitled *The Police Cycle Training Doctrine*. When it was revealed the booklet would cost thousands of pounds to produce, the Taxpayers' Alliance waded in and questioned the wisdom of spending so much money on a pamphlet which, when you really got down to it, was 'How to ride a bike'. You can't fool the Taxpayers' Alliance, you know.

'I've no doubt that the people behind this are well-intentioned but it is bonkers,' fumed the Alliance's spokeswoman Susie Squire. 'I think the booklet is slightly insulting the intelligence of bobbies and you have to ask how necessary this is. We believe that police forces should focus their resources on front-line policing.'

It's easy to see her point. The draft *Doctrine* contained some real pearls of cycling wisdom, including advice on how to brake, to wear padded shorts for 'in-saddle comfort' and a diagram explaining how to tackle particularly tricky junctions. Officers were also warned not to tackle suspects while still 'engaged with the cycle'.

The furore at the perceived profligacy of the police was so intense that London Mayor Boris Johnson decided to have his tuppence worth. 'I think you can do this kind of thing much, much more cheaply,' he told BBC Radio 4's *Today* programme.

ACPO were forced to admit it was a fair cop and agreed to shelve plans for their bobbies' bicycling bible, promising to spend the money saved on new handcuffs and stuff.

IT'LL ALL COME OUT
IN THE WASH
USA, 2009

Cycling has many purposes including, to name but a fleeting few, getting from A to B quicker than the pedestrians who favour the pavement, getting fit and healthy and, of course, providing grown men with a reasonably credible excuse to wear Lycra in public.

Washing your clothes is not traditionally one of them. Not until 2009, that is, when boffins at the Massachusetts Institute of Technology (MIT) across the pond unveiled the prototype of a revolutionary new device that cunningly combined the joys of cycling and the global dilemma of how to do the weekly laundry.

The premise for the concept was simple. Washing clothes in developing countries can be a bit of a bugger, what with the lack of electricity, water supplies and the latest machine from Hotpoint, and yet pedal power and basic parts, such as discarded oil drums, are readily available.

The eureka moment was almost upon our MIT students, and after a brief 15 hours in bed they came up with their 'Bicilavadora' (cleverly combining the Spanish words for bike and washing), a drum mounted on a frame and powered by a bicycle chain. The clothes would get as clean as you were prepared to pedal. The big selling points of the Bicilavadora were, of course, that it did not need electricity to shift those stubborn stains and the basic parts needed to repair and maintain it could be sourced locally.

The eggheads tested their innovative design in 2009 at an orphanage near Lima in Peru and, credit where it's due, it worked an absolute treat. The only problem was convincing the home's resident teenage boys of the need to wash their clothes on a weekly rather than biannual basis.

There are many more, slightly less philanthropic uses of pedal power. In 2012 the Cottage Lodge hotel in the New Forest installed a bicycle-powered television in one of its rooms, and it's now possible to buy a static bike with a blender attached to the handlebars should, presumably, you have an insatiable urge for a mango and passion fruit smoothie while in the saddle.

In 2013, however, American Edward Belden took it a step even further when he opened an ice-cream parlour, the 'Peddler's Creamery', in Los Angeles, freezing all of his delicious homemade offerings by pedal power alone.

'Bicycling is something I've been interested in since I was a kid,' Eddie panted. 'And I've been into ice cream since high school. My first job was at a Baskin-Robbins. I've been trying to figure out how to put those things together.'

If the idea was to catch on and customers forced to freeze their own 99s, America could be well on its way to solving its growing obesity crisis.

A BIZARRE BABY BUMP

FRANCE, 2009

Crashing your bike is generally very bad news indeed. However sunny your disposition, it's hard to crack a smile after you've plummeted painfully onto the tarmac, conducted an impromptu reverse skin graft on your knees and given the dentist one less tooth to worry about.

So when Kate Mansbridge went on a cycling holiday in the French Pyrenees in 2009, crashing her bike was definitely not part of her plans. Kate was no novice on two wheels, but things went rather awry when a runaway car ploughed into her on a narrow rural lane, and the poor girl was sent flying.

'I suddenly saw a navy blue Peugeot 106 careering towards us and it started spinning,' she said. 'I can remember thinking, "Oh my God, that's going to hit me and it's going to really hurt." Then it hit me, throwing me into the air before I landed face down on the tarmac, fighting for breath.

'I knew I'd broken both my legs, although I had no idea of the extent, both my shoulders were dislocated. I knew from my nursing training not to move, so I lay there face down. After they strapped a spinal board to me they flipped me over and that's when everyone gasped – I had two big open fractures across both my thighs – there was blood and bone hanging out of me. Things were so bad that my friend travelled with me in the helicopter so he could be with me if I didn't make it.'

Even worse was to follow as Kate also suffered a stroke that necessitated brain surgery. It's at this point you're probably wondering how this particular tale takes a turn for the better, but it did in the shape of her daughter, Ruby.

Mercifully Kate was not pregnant at the time of the crash. In fact, the doctors had told her she could never conceive after she had experienced early menopause in her late twenties, but her Pyrenees prang had a rather miraculous side effect: the severe head trauma she experienced produced a chemical change in her brain and in turn rebooted her menstrual cycle. And so, three years later and without even a whiff of IVF, Kate had a very welcome bun in the oven.

'While on the one hand, my legs were smashed to pieces and I was initially told I'd never walk again, on the other, the most extraordinary and incredible thing happened to me,' she said. 'It meant I was able to conceive my daughter Ruby, the daughter I'd always wanted. So while it was the worst thing that ever happened to me, it also turned out to be the best thing that had ever happened to me as well.

'Motherhood has been a revelation to me. Sometimes it's exhausting and frustrating, but it's also such a precious, wonderful gift and I know and appreciate that so much more, as I so nearly lost everything.'

Our ultimately uplifting story is, however, not quite complete. Kate may have rediscovered her ability to reproduce after her French fall but after undergoing brain surgery, she also woke up with a rare condition known as 'Foreign Accent Syndrome' and spoke with a South African accent. She was also able to speak fluent French in spite of it being years since she had gained her French A Level.

CHINA'S INVENTIVE VIGILANTE

CHINA, 2009

Sadly there are precious few examples of two-wheeled crime fighters in popular culture. Inspector Morse may or may not have kept a dusty penny-farthing in his shed, and there are rumours that Luther might have owned a Chopper in his youth, but the truth is our screens are rarely troubled by ne'er-do-wells being brought to justice by bikes.

It's a shame, because cycles are incredibly versatile crime-fighting tools. They are of course custom made for high-speed pursuits of miscreants, particularly on traffic-choked urban streets, but they're also excellent for casually carrying surveillance equipment, surreptitiously following suspects and getting to and from the local police station.

In 2009, an anonymous Chinese chap added to the humble cycle's crime-fighting credentials with a spot of inspired thief-busting, which mercifully did make it to our screens courtesy of local CCTV.

The scene is the city of Wenzhou and a young lady has just had her purse snatched by two likely lads on a scooter. She screams for help as the thieves speed off, and we now cut to the CCTV footage of the street along which the duo have chosen to make their escape.

There's a cyclist heading idly towards the scene of the crime and he stops when he hears the woman's cry. He dismounts his bike but seems uninterested in the unfolding events, apparently checking his handlebars and paying no attention to the approaching scooter. It is only when the thieves come into shot that he reacts, picking up his bike and throwing it square into the fleeing criminals as they come into range. Unsurprisingly, having a bike suddenly launched at their faces causes the pair of pilferers to experience an abrupt and hilarious crash, skidding along the tarmac for a few yards before grinding to a painful halt.

Good shot, son. The heroic bystander then proceeds to stride down the street purposefully towards the two prone crooks – whether to retrieve his bike or the stolen purse is unclear – but the dastardly duo are jolly angry at what's just occurred and jump up ready for a dust-up. It is at this point that our bike-throwing vigilante decides that discretion is the better part of valour, he's done quite enough amateur crime fighting for one day, and beats a rapid and probably wise retreat.

A local TV station subsequently tracked down our have-a-go hero, who agreed to be interviewed about the incident. Sadly it was all in Chinese, so we have absolutely no idea what they were talking about.

A POSTHUMOUS PROJECTILE

AUSTRALIA, 2009

Back in 2002, the good folk of New South Wales in Australia were mulling over the vexed issue of litter thrown from cars, and for four weeks adverts ran on state radio and television urging motorists to refrain from simply winding down their windows and ejecting their accumulated flotsam and jetsam onto the open road.

The genius element to the campaign was the slogan, 'Don't be a tosser.' Geddit? Those crazy Aussies, eh? To be fair it caught on and the pithy, but ever-so-slightly rude anti-littering epitaph even found its way over to the UK a decade later, when British drivers were urged to stop despoiling the highways and byways of this green and pleasant land.

Sorry, back to cycling. Unwelcome emissions from passing motorcars are a potential danger to all cyclists. An empty drink can, a discarded burger box or an unwanted copy of *Pigeon Fancier Monthly* can all do a bit of damage in the wrong hands, never mind besmirching the countryside, and riders have to be wary of any vehicle that passes with its windows down.

Pity then a Chinese 16-year-old by the name of Yun Tsui as he innocently pedalled his way home. The teenager was not far from his front door when he heard a car approaching at speed from behind, and before he could give it a second thought the motor had overtaken him.

As it did so, the door on the passenger side of the car suddenly opened. Mercifully, Yun wasn't wiped out by the door itself, but seconds later he was rather inconvenienced by what emerged from it, a large package thrown by one of the occupants of the car, which knocked him out of the saddle and left him unconscious on the side of the road.

When Yun came round, he was understandably curious as to what had been the cause of his misfortune. He began to unwrap the offending projectile and was more than a little disturbed when he realised it was a woman's corpse. The dead weight that had done for our teenage cyclist really was a dead weight.

The Chinese police raced to the unpleasant scene, and speculated that the deceased lady had been the victim of a fatal traffic accident in the nearby city of Dongyang and whoever was in the car was clumsily attempting to get rid of the evidence.

Yun was, of course, shaken up in more ways than one by his experience. 'My nephew is very upset,' said his uncle, clearly a master of understatement. 'A car passed and a package came flying out of the door. It had a dead woman inside.'

Looking on the bright side, at least the body wasn't inside a coffin. Now that really would have hurt.

BATTERIES NOT INCLUDED

HOLLAND AND FRANCE, 2010

An essential part of the bicycle's DNA is the reliance on human power. Bikes come in many different shapes and sizes, but our two-wheeled friends are united in their contempt for anything resembling an engine. Nature may abhor a vacuum, but cycles absolutely hate motors.

Which is why the world of professional cycling was rocked to its foundations in 2010, when high-profile Swiss rider Fabian Cancellara was accused of using a motor concealed in his bike frame to help him win the Tour of Flanders and the Paris–Roubaix race.

The accusation of what amounted to racing heresy was made by former professional rider Davide Cassani. He stated in a video posted on YouTube that a small motor could easily be hidden in the seat tube of a bike and the ignition switch located in the handlebars, and then showed clips of Cancellara in action, claiming there were moments his dramatic increases in speed could only have been achieved with, ahem, 'extra help'.

The indignant Swiss was quick to rebuff the accusations. 'In fact it was pretty funny at first but it is such a big story that it's no longer the case,' he told the Belgian newspaper *Het Nieuwsblad*. 'It's a sad story and really outrageous. Don't worry, my accomplishments are the result of hard work. It's so stupid I'm speechless. I've never had batteries on my bike.'

The problem was there were already rumours of unnamed riders using a new engine called the Gruber Assist that could surreptitiously generate 100 watts of additional power, and when the Cancellara 'story' broke, fear mixed with suspicion and everyone got rather hot under the collar.

It's important to stress here that the governing body, Union Cycliste Internationale (UCI), decided Cancellara was innocent and refused to investigate the unproven slurs, but the allegation alone raised the spectre of motorised cheating in a sport that was still wrestling with the ongoing issue of doping.

The worrying aspect of the tale was the realisation that the authorities were in no real position to catch out potential 'motor cheats'. 'If there's been some kind of fraud, there's no way of proving it,' admitted the UCI's technical chief Jean Wauthier. 'Certainly we're going to have to speed up our research so we can scan all competition bikes in a quick and efficient way. Up till now, such controls simply haven't been used.'

GOING UNDERGROUND
JAPAN, 2010

For most urban commuters who eschew public transport, the search for a parking space is a continual nightmare. It doesn't matter whether you're driving a petite hatchback or a more capacious estate car, city centres are becoming increasingly hostile to the internal combustion engine, and these days there just isn't enough space for everyone's motor.

This growing animosity to cars has proven something of a boom to bikes, with the advent of increasing numbers of cycling lanes. The modern metropolitan area loves two wheels and many cyclists are now confidently predicting it will not be long before cities become their exclusive preserve.

The only problem is where exactly do you put all the bikes once you've banished the car and everyone's pedalled into town? All the car parks will obviously be transformed into giant concrete bike racks, following government legislation, but what happens when they're full?

Space has always been at a premium on the crowded streets of Tokyo, and although bikes have long ruled the roost over their four-wheeled rivals in the Japanese capital, the question of where to store them while everyone's diligently working at their desks has been frequently raised. In 2010 the city's transport chiefs came up with an ingenious answer and the world's first automated underground bike storage facility was brought into service.

Buried 36ft (11m) beneath the city's bustling pavements, the ECO-Cycle system was essentially a vast, steel-walled cylinder capable of holding up to 200 bikes. At street level riders parked their cycles in the designated drop-off area, the bikes were then clamped in place before a robotic arm whisked them off to their subterranean bolthole. The whole process took a mere eight seconds, and when the rider wanted their machine back, they simply swiped a card or tapped in an ID code and their bike was mechanically returned ready for their journey home.

The ECO-Cycle system was such a hit that by 2013 there were 43 of them across Japan, and although they didn't exactly come cheap at over £1 million each, they were (their manufacturers proudly pointed out) earthquake-resistant. Which was nice.

The number of reported thefts of bicycles in Tokyo unsurprisingly plummeted following the introduction of the ECO-Cycle, as the machines were rather difficult to pilfer now they were safely cocooned beneath the city's streets. The only downside of the scheme was the number of erstwhile bike thieves who were subsequently forced to turn to busking and street mime to make ends meet.

BROUGHT DOWN TO EARTH
USA, 2011

It was back in 1973 that Alan Bean enjoyed his unprecedented pedal in space (see 'Out of this World', page 98) but fellow astronaut Tim Kopra found bicycling and going into orbit far less compatible 38 years later when he was left to curse his love of two wheels.

A former Army helicopter pilot and veteran of both the American campaigns in Iraq, Kopra was part of the crew that blasted off in the *Endeavour* shuttle in July 2009, spending three months aboard the International Space Station.

Almost as soon as he touched down, he was selected for the mission on *Discovery* in February 2011 and he also got the nod to make the two space walks scheduled for the trip. A popular boy, our Tim.

After 20 months of intensive, arduous training and three threats of divorce from his lonely, disgruntled missus, Kopra was in tip-top shape and ready for lift-off.

Five weeks before the big day, however, Tim made the fateful decision to go out for a nice relaxing bike ride, which ended with him breaking his hip. NASA refused to release details of exactly what happened or what he hit, but Kopra's big adventure was over.

The shuttle, of course, could not be delayed, NASA turned to the subs' bench and they left on schedule and without him.

'It was obviously a disappointment for Tim to not be available for this upcoming launch window,' said chief astronaut Peggy Whitson after hearing the news, 'but he understands very well that we have to be prepared to fly.'

To rub salt into the wound, the shuttle that Kopra missed was the STS-133. The iconic aircraft made just two more trips into space before it was retired by NASA in 2011, meaning accident-prone Tim will now never get the chance to go up in the shuttle again.

Kopra's career as an astronaut was far from over, however. Indeed, between March and June 2016 he served as Commander on Expedition 47 of the International Space Station, alongside our very own Tim Peake.

SOZZLED IN THE SADDLE

USA, 2011

Cycling poses many eternal questions. Can you, for example, ever truly call yourself a cyclist if you can't fix a puncture? Are there any situations when it's justified to run a red light? And exactly how long is it acceptable, in polite society, to wear your Lycra shorts after jumping out of the saddle?

Another long-standing and thorny subject for riders is the issue of the demon drink. Is cycling after a few alcopops a mortal sin, or merely a bit of a laugh? Is a slightly unsteady pedal home after three pints of Guinness at your local OK or not? Exactly how much damage can you do on two wheels while suffering from an artificially enhanced sense of self-confidence, impaired peripheral vision and a burning desire to tell everyone how much you love them?

Different places have different rules about riding under the influence. Take the American city of Pittsburgh, for example, where it is most definitely an offence to be in charge of a bicycle after one too many tipples. They're really quite clear about that over in Pittsburgh, stating as it does in their big book of rules that '... [e]very person riding a pedalcycle upon a roadway ... shall be subject to all of the duties applicable to the driver of a vehicle.'

Strange then that 59-year-old James Takos should choose this particular conurbation to become three sheets to the wind, jump into the saddle, and shout loudly, 'Drunk people shouldn't ride bicycles!' before slamming into the kerb, flipping himself over the handlebars and knocking himself unconscious. He was clearly not the sharpest tool in the box.

What's particularly strange about this strange tale, however, is that James' behaviour isn't even the strangest part. Oh no, it all went even more peculiar after Pittsburgh's finest finished their doughnuts and showed up to clean up the mess.

The first officer on the scene was one Charles Bosetti, who concluded that since the only damage James had done was to himself, and as his head was still bleeding profusely, he would treat the incident as a medical issue and no more. The second copper to turn up went by the name of Lisa Luncinski and she wanted to throw the book at James. Remarkably the two law enforcement colleagues ended up facing each other in court over James' well-lubricated little bike ride.

It all got rather acrimonious. 'I told him we were not going to arrest him if he agreed to go to the hospital,' Bosetti told the judge. 'It was obvious he was impaired by alcoholic beverages,' countered Luncinski. 'I could smell him from 20ft [6.1m] away.'

Without going into too much detail, Luncinski went behind Bosetti's back, found out from the doctors that James was indeed absolutely smashed and charged him with driving under the influence. Bosetti came back with the argument that James had only admitted to being bladdered *after* being told he wasn't going to be charged, and any subsequent attempt to charge him was an infringement of his rights as a suspect.

The judge sighed wearily as he only had ten minutes to get to the first tee and decided to let James off with the lesser charges of public intoxication and disorderly conduct and sent him on his way. On foot.

The squabbling between the two officers was far from over. 'She thinks I blow off arrests,' Bosetti said. 'I believe she railroads people.' Luncinski replied: 'I respond to my 911 calls like they're my family members calling for the police. He does not.' The duo were sent to mediation in an attempt to reduce tensions, but only brought the department into further disrepute after they became involved in a shootout in reception.

MILLAR'S ILLEGAL MILESTONE

ENGLAND, 2011

It's an increasingly common complaint these days that the cult of celebrity is getting rather out of hand. The modern era's adulation of anyone deemed famous is seemingly unquestioning and if you've appeared on the telly, got more than 10,000 YouTube subscribers, or once found yourself in the same room as Kim Kardashian, you are elevated onto a pedestal far above the hordes of the great unwashed.

Cycling has never been short of a star or two, and in the days before Messrs Wiggins and Kenny, Froome and Cavendish, one of the biggest names in the business was Scotland's David Millar, a former British national road race champion and the winner of four stages of the Tour de France.

In 2011 Dave released his autobiography, and to generate a bit of publicity for his new book he organised a ride around Richmond Park in London with some pals and local cyclists. Aside from possible collisions with the park's numerous resident deer, what could possibly go wrong?

Millar completed the 6¾-mile (10.8km) loop of Richmond Park in a record 13 minutes and 35 seconds. If you've not got a calculator to hand, that means he pedalled the course at an average speed of just under 30mph (48.3km/h), and to his credit, he managed to avoid ploughing into any of Bambi's relatives.

The problem was that the speed limit for the park is 20mph (32.2km/h), and Millar had rather publicly incriminated himself with his promotional stunt. A rapid and grovelling response was required. 'I've written to the Royal Parks and apologised profusely,' Millar said. 'I explained that it was all down to my naivety. I had no idea of the rules. I've lived in France and Spain for so long, where this wouldn't be a problem, that I didn't even think to check.'

The Royal Parks considered the letter. Dave's guilt was undeniable and they could have instigated legal proceedings, but thought twice when someone pointed out that Millar was, you know, a bit famous. You can't prosecute famous people, can you? They quietly dropped the case and said no more about it.

That might have been the end of our tale, but two years later a teenager was riding down Sawyers Hill in the very same Richmond Park, and with the help of the slope and some vigorous pedalling managed to clock up an illegal speed of 37mph (59.5km/h).

The Royal Parks were furious and when someone pointed out that the teenager was not famous in any shape or form – he'd only ever played second sheep in the school Nativity play – they decided to throw the book at him. The poor lad got a six-month conditional discharge for speeding and was ordered to pay a £15 victim surcharge and £85 court costs.

THE HEIGHT OF INGENUITY

CUBA, 2012

Cycling has proved a fertile area for those whose mission in life is to see their names in the *Guinness Book of World Records*. Getting into the book is a moot claim to fame when you consider Britain's Steve Mesure made the grade in 2013 after creating the world's biggest whoopee cushion, while Croatia's Krunoslav Budiselic was included after his Herculean achievement of fitting 150 socks on his right foot (we're honestly not making this up) but, hey, it still beats trainspotting as a hobby.

The number of record-breaking feats you can accomplish in the saddle is almost limitless, and then there are also extreme bicycle modifications, such as building bigger, longer, faster or heavier bikes than ever seen before, in an attempt to join the 'elite' Guinness World Records club.

In 2012 a Cuban chap called Felix Guirola decided to make his bid to become a bicycle record-breaker. Felix opted for the 'world's tallest bike' category, and after months toiling away with his blowtorch in a workshop in Havana, he proudly emerged with his creation, an 18ft (5m 49cm) monster that would give the faint-hearted rider severe vertigo.

'I've never been much of a cyclist,' Felix confessed, 'but I really like riding tall bikes. I don't know if this interests Cubans but it interests me. This is my hobby.' His other half was noticeably less enthusiastic. 'I say sometimes it's like an obsession,' Mrs Guirola said through gritted teeth.

'It is always about bicycles and each passing day it gets a little bit taller.'

Marital tensions aside, Felix should have been on cloud nine, but his face dropped when someone pointed out to him that, according to Guinness World Records, the tallest bike was actually an 18ft 2½in (5m 55cm) behemoth built by Canadian pastor Terry Goertzen and ridden without stabilisers over a distance of 328 yards (300m) at the North Kildonan Mennonite Brethren Church in Winnipeg in 2004.

'Nobody ever told me anything,' replied a clearly dejected Felix as he scurried off to his workshop clutching more metal piping and his trusty blowtorch. To rub salt into the wound, the bar was legitimately raised in 2013 when American Richie Trimble pedalled proudly around Los Angeles on a lofty machine that stretched the tape measure to 20ft 2½in (6m 16cm). You could almost hear Felix sobbing across the Gulf of Mexico.

Other oversized record-breaking bikes include the extraordinarily elongated beast built by members of the Mijl Van Mares Werkploeg workers collective in the Netherlands in 2011, a cycle that measured a staggering 117ft 5½in (35m 80cm) from front wheel to back, while it was just over the border in Belgium in 2015 that Jeff Peeters unveiled his two-wheeled beast that tipped the scales at a record 1,896lb (860kg).

'It was a great experience,' Jeff said after pedalling his gargantuan contraption. 'I used some axle shafts from old machines. And there were some new pipes, too. Some materials were new. It's high and it's not very stable.'

After spending six months working on the massive bike, the same could have been said of Jeff himself.

THE BIG CHILL
ANTARCTICA, 2012

Cyclists and snow are rarely happy bedfellows. Even the most devoted rider will think twice about setting out for an invigorating pedal on a winter's morning if, on drawing the bedroom curtains, they're confronted by masses of the white stuff. Bikes are tough, but even they would follow the birds south for the winter if they had a choice.

Which is why, until 2012 at least, successive generations of intrepid explorers had never deigned to use our two-wheeled friends en route to the South Pole, opting instead to load up with Winalot and let the husky take the strain.

It all changed, however, in the name of Sport Relief when *Blue Peter* presenter Helen Skelton embarked on an ambitious 500-mile (800km) expedition into the wintery wilderness of Antarctica for charity, 103 miles (166km) of which our indomitable children's TV presenter planned to travel in the saddle.

'I've lost count of the number of people who have told me a push-bike won't work in Antarctica and that I am setting myself up for a fall,' she confessed before pulling on her thermals and setting off. 'It's become a joke among the Icelandic Arctic truck drivers who provide logistical support here. They think I am bonkers.'

Braving temperatures as low as -54.4°F (-48°C), Helen began her bid to reach the South Pole on 4 January and it soon became apparent the truckers might have a point.

'We had a ten-hour day yesterday with the bikes,' she recorded in her diary for *The Daily Telegraph*.

'The first part of the day went well. We covered 10 miles [16.1km] quite quickly then we hit some soft snow and that was game over for the bikes. We ended up pushing them for the last 6 miles [9.7km] to make sure we made the miles for the day. This morning the snow conditions were no better so we had to push our bikes again, not what you need in minus 23 [°C/-9.4°F] as you get colder quicker. So we took the decision to swap onto the skis, but progress has been slow, mainly as I'm not much of a cross-country skier.

'The hardness of the snow the nearer you get to the Pole gets softer. In fact its texture, in parts, is just like sand and the bike wheels simply can't get any traction or grip.'

Helen, though, was nothing if not plucky and after 18 days in the freezer she finally reached the South Pole, proudly pedalling the final few miles just to prove a point to the sceptics.

PLAY YOUR CARD RIGHT
ISRAEL, 2012

It's all well and good manufacturing a bicycle frame from bamboo (see 'You've Been Framed', page 153) but the process still involves the massacre of an innocent plant, cruelly cut down in its prime. The green credentials of the bamboo bike are moot.

It would surely be far more environmentally friendly if we could avoid such carnage and rather recycle what we have already harvested from the natural world. An affordable, recycled cardboard bicycle maybe?

Thank God then for Israeli-based engineer Izhar Gafni and his backers ERB, who unveiled just such a wondrous contraption in 2012 with the bold promise their prototype was going to change the world.

'Like Henry Ford who made the car available to anybody,' enthused Gafni, 'this bike is going to be cheap and available to any child in the world, including children in Africa who walk dozens of miles to school every day.'

Big words, but you've got to hand it to Gafni and his friends, who did, indeed, manage to layer and form the recycled cardboard in such a way that it was strong enough to carry the weight of an adult. Not a morbidly obese giant, admittedly, but a normal-sized grown-up nonetheless.

The design team also successfully negotiated the nagging problem that cardboard has a tendency to get soggy in the rain, coating the frame of their bike with a waterproof resin before applying a fetching coat of paint. Job done.

Each bike cost just £10 to manufacture, and everyone connected to the project was jolly pleased.

'The biggest challenge of the Cardboard Bike Project was to learn and develop a whole new know-how of cardboard,' an ERB spokesman gushed. 'The challenge was to take the cardboard material and pass it through a set of treatments to replace the raw materials of plastic, wood or metal.' Nothing is impossible if you have patience and you are persistent.

'Cardboard technologies is all about making a better world for us to live in by two main principles: creating the ability to produce almost any daily product from at least 95 per cent recycled materials and building auto production lines with a simple post-production assembly that will be performed by people with difficulties or disabilities.'

The day when cyclists can build their own bikes at home from empty cornflake boxes or discarded All-Bran packets may be some way off just yet, but it's a tantalising prospect.

JUST MARRIED!
NEW ZEALAND, 2012

The honeymoon is traditionally a long overdue opportunity for a newly-wed couple to have some precious time alone, recover from the trials and tribulations of organising their recent nuptials, forget about how much money they've just wasted on champagne and vol-au-vents, and slag off their new in-laws.

It's also, perhaps, a once-in-a-lifetime opportunity for some personal pampering and indulgence before reality bites, the patter of tiny feet arrives and the happy couple are inevitably reduced to emotional, physical and financial wrecks.

And yet not all new couples conform to this convention, and after tying the knot, Kat and Steve Turner turned their back on the luxury hotel and the sun loungers and set off on an epic, potentially record-breaking tandem ride from New Zealand to London.

Worryingly, Kat had never ridden a bike for more than a few yards before embarking on this bizarre matrimonial challenge, but after a few quick lessons the Turners set off from Christchurch on New Zealand's South Island in May 2012, and by the end of the year they'd reached Darwin and the north coast of Australia.

'The first four months of this trip were so hard,' Kat admitted. 'We cycled through gallons of rain and waves of gales. My feet felt like they were constantly soaked and at times I wanted to give up so much, so that I could enjoy a beer and good company with friends or the warmth of a fire or a Sunday roast at Mum's or a belly-aching laugh with my brother or a family knees-up in Plymouth. And, dare I say it, even working in a dry office felt appealing at times.'

A few angry dogs, giant lizards and hungry rats slowed their initial progress, but after beginning the Asian leg of their grand tour, Mr and Mrs Turner finally felt they were getting to grips with the task, if not each other.

'At first we were not sure whether we could do what we were planning to do but now that we have completed six months and the Australian Outback we feel much more confident that we can do this,' said Steve. 'If we do, it will be the most amazing achievement. We have found the first months very hard and we haven't had the energy or the contacts to do very much other than cycle, which isn't exactly a traditional way of enjoying a honeymoon.'

Quite. The plucky duo kept on pedalling and pedalling despite their trials and tribulations, and in April 2014, they were finally back in the UK after visiting 22 countries over 699 days. In total, they had cycled 19,263 miles (31,000km) on their faithful tandem, which it transpired they had nicknamed 'Hooch'.

'It has been a fantastic journey and an amazing experience,' Kat said after catching her breath. 'There were so many people we met that made it special. It has certainly made the world seem like a much less scary place. But it was extremely difficult too, and not as romantic as you imagine your honeymoon might be – most of our nights were spent in a tiny two-person tent rubbing cream into each other's sore bits.'

After a few days back at home, the couple soon embarked on another seemingly insurmountable challenge, otherwise known as writing their long-overdue wedding present thank you cards.

JAMIE'S ROAD TO NOWHERE

THAILAND–UK, 2012

Static bikes are a contentious issue in the cycling community. Traditionalists fume that pedalling without actually moving anywhere is an aberration, an affront to the very essence of cycling, while forward-thinking two-wheel devotees counter that it beats getting chased by dogs or knocked over by idiots in BMWs.

Others, such as tennis coach Jamie McDonald, eagerly embrace both disciplines.

Jamie began 2012 on something of a mad mission. His first challenge began in January when he and his trusty bike set off from the Thai capital Bangkok, his ambitious aim to reach his hometown of Gloucester by pedal power alone. It took him ten months to cycle the 14,000 miles (22,531km) back to the UK, but after a journey that took him through Iran and Iraq, to name but two of the more dangerous countries he traversed, Jamie arrived home safely.

Most sane people would have enjoyed a well-earned spot of R&R after completing such a feat, but Jamie was restless, and less than a month after his return he decided to target the world record for continuous pedalling on a static bike, a remarkable milestone of 224 hours, 24 minutes and 24 exhausting seconds set by Patrizio Sciroli of Italy in 2011.

In December, he strapped himself on and began pumping his legs once again. The rules stated he had to cycle for a minimum of 22 hours per day at an average of 12mph

(19.3km/h), but the masochist in Jamie was in evidence once more as he limited himself to just 90 minutes' sleep rather than the two hours he was allowed.

After ten days in the saddle, he had smashed Sciroli's record, but powered on and eventually set a new mark of 290 hours and 18 minutes on the bike. 'I've been cycling for 11 days straight, am I hallucinating?' he gasped when it was all finally over. 'No, this is for real. This is just mind-blowing.'

In September 2013 Guinness World Records got in touch to confirm Jamie's ordeal had officially made the book, but he wasn't at home to receive the good news, indisposed as he was on a coast-to-coast run across Canada – the potentially suicidal equivalent of 200 marathons in just 275 days – in an attempt to set another record.

The expression 'glutton for punishment' doesn't even come close.

CARRY ON, DOCTOR
USA, 2012

Bicycles boast a long, proud history of aiding the medical profession, from their deployment on the bloody battlefields of World War One and their tireless work with dowdy district nurses in remote, rural areas to the modern cycle response units that today reassuringly patrol our cities (see 'An Unlikely Medical Hero', page 133).

A more unlikely and comical collaboration between a bicycle and the medical community, however, came to light in the American state of Louisiana in 2012, when a Dr Catherine Baucom, a dedicated oncologist, suddenly found herself in rather desperate need of some two-wheeled assistance.

A surgeon at a hospital in the state capital of Baton Rouge, Doc Baucom set off for work as usual one sunny morning in August. She drove onto the Interstate but a pile-up a few miles up the road prematurely curtailed her journey and she found herself stuck in traffic. Due in surgery and with the clock ticking, an increasingly anxious Baucom decided to pull off the Interstate and drive to a nearby friend's house.

Luckily her pal did have an alternative form of transport, but it turned out to be his seven-year-old daughter's pink bike, complete with a pink Disney helmet. Remembering her Hippocratic Oath, Baucom didn't blink an eye and before you could say stabilisers, she was back on the road and pedalling furiously towards the hospital.

At six feet tall, our unstoppable doctor wasn't exactly well suited to her new ride, but she persevered and after a couple of miles of uncomfortable cycling she came across a police patrol that had been despatched to manage the aftermath of the Interstate accident. 'I rode up on this bright pink bike wearing a princess helmet,' Baucom said. 'They probably thought I was a mental patient. I said, "Look, I've got to operate, can you let me through?"'

They did and 'escorted' Baucom safely and on time to the operating theatre, the climax of a frenetic rush to surgery. It would have been less frantic had the police actually given her a lift to the hospital rather than following her and her pint-sized bike with their lights flashing.

FROOME'S AFRICAN ADVENTURE
FRANCE (VIA AFRICA), 2013

We've already enjoyed a few laughs at the expense of the Tour de France riders who've had the misfortune to be involved in canine collisions in the past (see 'Who Let the Dogs Out?', page 149) but our four-legged friends wouldn't have worried 2013 Tour champion Chris Froome, judging by his own experiences of the animal kingdom growing up in Africa.

The Team Sky star was raised in the rural highlands north of the Kenyan capital Nairobi, and a misplaced pooch would have been a picnic compared to the far more fearsome African beasts he regularly encountered in his formative years.

The sight of wild lions on the prowl while he was out training was a common one for the youngster, but it was a disgruntled hippopotamus that came closest to bringing Froome's career to a premature end. 'Growing up in Africa has its colourful times,' he said in 2011. 'I was fishing one day and a hippo came out of the river and chased me up an embankment. To most people in Europe, it's something so foreign. There are many places in Africa I've been riding my bike and you come across animals.'

The danger did not only lurk outdoors, and a slither of snakes billeted at the family house mercifully never turned on the future Tour champion. 'Mum wasn't a fan but wanted to encourage us learning, so she let us keep them in the house,' recalled older brother Jeremy. 'We had about 50 in the house. Chris had two pythons, Rocky and Shandy, he absolutely loved.'

The animal kingdom, however, was not the only threat to the teenager. The fields around the family home were riddled with bilharzia, a debilitating parasitic infection that can affect growth in children, and Froome and both his brothers suffered bouts of the disease growing up.

And then there were the manmade hazards, including concealed metal spikes and HGVs.

The metal spike went right through his foot during a family holiday. 'It needed a hacksaw to cut it off and though it must have been excruciatingly painful,' said Jeremy, 'he never complained, just stayed quiet. That's Chris. People see a quiet, polite soul but inside he's fiery and strong.'

The lorries were more fun, as Froome hung onto the back of the speeding trucks while out on his bike, but it is something of a minor miracle he never hit one of the numerous potholes or dead dogs and finished his ride lying in a ditch.

Compared to these childhood challenges, winning the Tour probably seemed like a breeze.

THE SKY'S THE LIMIT
ENGLAND, 2013

We have already explored the bicycle's key role in helping man get airborne at the start of the 20th century (see 'The Wright Stuff', page 33), but in recent years the cycling fraternity has been making a concerted effort to muscle in on the aeroplane's dominance of the skies.

The concept of a flying bike had tantalised and teased frustrated inventors for decades, but in 2013 it finally became a reality when two British designers unveiled their 'Paravelo', an innovation which they boldly promised would revolutionise commuting forever.

Powered by a large fan connected to a bio-fuel engine and mounted on two extra supporting wheels at the back of the bike, the Paravelo achieved lift-off courtesy of a parachute attached to the frame. It wasn't a million miles away from a microlight, and video evidence proved it definitely could fly.

'We live in Kingston upon Thames on the outskirts of London, two minutes' walk from the birthplace of the Sopwith Aviation Company, which built the Sopwith Camel for the Royal Air Force during the First World War,' explained co-creator John Foden. 'We were enchanted by the connection between cycling and the birth of powered flight. The Wright brothers were former bicycle mechanics, so we designed the Paravelo to recapture that pioneering era.'

Foden and his fellow boffin Yannick Read claimed their machine could reach heights of 4,000ft (1,220m) and stay airborne for up to three hours. It could also be folded up and stored, they enthused, meaning you could fly to work and then pop your Paravelo away neatly in the stationery cupboard. They were less forthcoming when asked what the hell you'd do should you find yourself 2,000ft (610m) above Grimsby town centre on a Tuesday morning and the engine stalls.

In the same year, a group of Czech chaps with white coats took a very different approach to the old 'flying bike' conundrum when they unveiled a prototype that did away altogether with the parachute, and instead gained elevation thanks to a series of six downward-facing fans welded to the cycle's frame.

They demonstrated their invention to reporters but, rather worryingly, did not have sufficient faith in their machine to put a real live person in the saddle, and flew the bike by remote control.

'Our main motivation in working on the project was neither profit nor commercial interest,' explained Ales Kobylik, 'but the fulfilment of our boyish dreams.'

Questions about safety features and the possibility of suffering a horrible death, however, were met with an embarrassed silence, and until some genius can come up with the answers, the future of flying bikes seems uncertain at best.

THE NEED FOR SPEED
FRANCE, 2013

Ever since the modern bicycle emerged in the late 19th century, people have been endeavouring to go faster and faster and then even faster still on two wheels. The pursuit of speed has, of course, resulted in countless crashes but it's also produced some amazing feats of engineering and moments of sheer undiluted madness.

The maddest of them all in the cycling speed stakes has to be Frenchman François Gissy, who clocked up a potentially fatal but admittedly impressive 163mph (262km/h) on his hydrogen peroxide-powered rocket bike in 2013, a new land speed record on a bicycle.

To put it into context, that's faster than the winner of the 3.30 at Kempton, an Andy Murray first serve or an Audi RS6 flat out. It's even faster than a politician on the campaign trail after they've just spotted a baby and a photographer in close proximity.

Gissy built his bike himself and then attached a reinforced storage tank filled with liquid hydrogen peroxide which, when mixed with a catalyst, produces oodles of steam which in turn provides the thrust. A GPS tracker on the handlebars recorded the ridiculous speed.

The Munchhouse Aerodrome in Alsace, France provided the setting for the attempt and after ensuring his will was in order and saying a few Hail Marys, Gissy flipped the switch and duly rocketed into the record books.

There's a problem though, isn't there? A rocket-powered bike doesn't exactly adhere to the principles of pedal power, and while he didn't technically convert his bicycle into a motorbike, his feat was not a muscular achievement.

The real distinction as the fastest man on two wheels, unadulterated by rockets, unaided by a tow from a fast car and without the help of a slipstream created by an advance vehicle, therefore belongs to Dutchman Sebastian Bowier.

Superb Seb set his record in September 2013 at Battle Mountain in Nevada in a specially designed recumbent bike shielded by an aerodynamic shell covered in the same coating used on Formula One cars, clocking an incredible top speed of 83.13mph (133.8km/h) courtesy of pedal power alone.

Bowier's amazing effort eclipsed the previous record set by Canadian Sam Whittingham four years earlier, but it was an unbelievably close-run thing, the Dutchman going just 0.311mph (0.5km/h) faster than his rival.

SHANGHAI HIGH RISE

CHINA, 2013

The Chinese have become addicted to building skyscrapers. They just can't get enough of throwing up taller and taller buildings, towering architectural reminders to the rest of the world that they'll be in charge soon and we'd better not forget it, thank you.

The imposing Shanghai World Financial Centre – an enticing blend of office space, shops and a luxury hotel – first opened its doors for business in 2008. At the time of the grand unveiling, it was officially the second tallest building in the world, but that didn't last long, and by 2016 it had been demoted to only ninth on the all-time list.

Still, it is impressive nonetheless: 101 floors, a dizzying 1,568ft 1⅓in (477m 96cm) tall and an impossible 2,754 steps just to get to the breathtaking observation deck on the 100th floor. You have to be mad to attempt it on foot.

Or, of course, on two wheels, but pedalling up skyscrapers is Krystian Herba's thing, and in March 2013 the Polish part-time PE teacher and part-time stunt rider pitched up at the SWFC (as the locals may call it) ready for his latest challenge.

He'd already knocked off the comparatively puny Rose Tower building in Dubai – a mere 2,040 steps over 91 floors – and now he'd come to show Shanghai what he could really do.

Now it's important to put this challenge, the kind of superhuman feat that Guinness World Records will actually recognise, into context. Herba is not allowed to put his feet down for the duration of the attempt and he's not allowed to touch the walls with his hands either. He simply has to keep pedalling up and up and up. On a bike with no seat, lest it unbalance him.

Impossible? Not for our Krystian, who successfully pedalled, bounced and balanced his bike all the way to the SWFC's 100th floor in a time of one hour, 21 minutes and 53 seconds.

'It is like asking a Himalayan climber why he is going to the mountains if he can simply stay at home,' Herba replied when quizzed why the hell he spent his spare time climbing skyscrapers on his bike. 'It's the strength and desire to be better and faster and to overcome, not only another record, but also weaknesses.'

Either that or he's claustrophobic and won't take the lift.

THE BICYCLE BANDITS

USA, 2013

We have already discussed how over the years law enforcement has taken to two wheels to catch crooks (see 'Bobbies on Bikes', page 169), but the criminal fraternity are also aware of pedal power, as these contrasting tales of audacious crooks prove.

There are, somewhat worryingly, countless stories of armed robberies in which the perpetrator makes his or her escape on a bike, but one of the most surreal was the stick-up at a branch of Bank of America in Georgia in 2013, a raid carried out by a man wearing a bright blonde wig. Inconspicuous is not the word that springs to mind.

'I noticed him right away' said one customer after the robbery, 'because when I walked in, I saw him sitting there. He had on the wig and he just kind of looked like a transsexual.'

The crook's disguise may have been poor, but what it lacked in subtlety he made up for with audacity, and after grabbing a bag of cash he calmly strolled out of the building and got into the saddle for a successful getaway. An oblivious security guard at the bank even held the door open for him as he made his exit.

The two-wheeled thief who targeted a Wells Fargo bank in Alaska two years earlier was not nearly so lucky. Things initially went to plan, but after leaving the bank with his ill-gotten gains, he was spotted pedalling away by a patrol car and the Old Bill gave chase. The crook made it a little further, but the game was up when the officer manoeuvred his car in front of the fleeing bicycle and the criminal was sent unceremoniously crashing over the bonnet.

'He ended in a heap with his money pouring out of his pack,' revealed Lt Dave Parker. 'It didn't hurt him at all. He popped up and ran away.'

It was merely a temporary reprieve as the officer slipped on his running shoes, chased the suspect down and slapped on the cuffs.

Natural hazards, however, can be as dangerous as police cars, as one criminal found out in 2009 when he walked into a Canadian petrol station near Niagara Falls wielding a butcher's knife and demanded the money.

The attendant wisely paid up but when the thief made off on his bicycle, he jumped into his car and followed him. The crook panicked and the bizarre game of cat and mouse came to an abrupt and painful end when he crashed head first into a tree.

The most idiotic attempt to escape justice on two wheels, though, has to be the American man who walked into a Walmart in Florida in 2012 and half-inched a 32in plasma TV, jumped on his bike and began pedalling. His new acquisition proved to be more hindrance than help and, unable to steer properly, he slammed into a police car and was promptly nicked.

IT'S NOT ALWAYS GOOD TO TALK

AUSTRALIA, 2013

One of cyclists' perennial gripes about motorists is their persistent and illegal use of mobile phones. It's impossible for drivers, they argue, to give the road their due care and attention while they're being bombarded by calls about PPI, arguing with their other halves or trying to order a pepperoni pizza.

It was back in 2003 that the UK banned the use of handheld mobiles behind the wheel, but other countries have gone even further to curtail potentially dangerous conversations on the road, and in certain states in Australia it also illegal to use your mobile while in the saddle.

It's a tough law but one that is enforced, as an anonymous female cyclist in a suburb of Adelaide discovered in 2013 when the eagle-eyed Old Bill spotted her chatting away on the phone while riding a bike. She was fined $110 for her two-wheeled transgression and sent on her way.

Hardly a 'strange tale' you cry, but we haven't yet touched upon the bike on which she committed her heinous crime, a homemade, multicoloured double-decker contraption, which really was a sight to behold.

Boasting a yellow 'lower' frame with a bright pink 'upper' frame avec wheels precariously welded on top, the cycle was powered by a long chain running at 45 degrees between the chain wheel at the top and the 'cassette' (the little 'toothy' metal circle) at the bottom rear. It was all topped off with some fetching beads cunningly woven between the spokes of the front wheel, and looked as psychedelic as it did potentially lethal.

'Cyclists are vulnerable road users,' intoned a straight-faced police spokesman after the unnamed woman was pulled over, 'and are reminded that the road rules also apply to them.'

How our cyclist actually managed to ride her bizarre bike and speak on the phone is something of a mystery, but perhaps she opted for her elevated pedalling position in order to get a better reception on her mobile.

CANADIAN
CARDBOARD CAPER

CANADA, 2013

Theft is the scourge of the urban cyclist's life, transforming a brief stop-off for a cinnamon latte and croissant into a heart-rending experience as they emerge from the coffee shop to discover their beloved wheels have disappeared.

The chances of successfully recovering their prized possession are usually as remote as Bouvet Island (look it up on a map), and while it might be unfair to suggest that the police don't prioritise searching for pilfered bikes, you'd definitely get laughed out of the station if you popped in and demanded to speak to the head of the crack Cycle Crime Unit.

Occasionally, however, the scales of justice do tip in the favour of the wronged rider, emotional reunions between man and machine do happen and stolen bikes are found.

One such serendipitous conclusion was reached in Toronto in 2013, when yet another bike was criminally separated from its lock and promptly nicked. The owner held out little hope of ever seeing it again but a few days later his friend – get this, a bicycle mechanic – spotted the missing bike chained to a metal post on the side of the street, and through the wonderful medium of the Internet (or, more specifically, Reddit) announced to his mate and the wider world that bikey was coming home.

The pair set about cutting the bike free from its new lock but rather than call it a day, they decided to rub their victory in the thief's face, leaving a cardboard cut-out of a bicycle in the exact same spot with a note attached.

'Dear Bike Thief,' it read. 'You rascal! You took my bike earlier this week and forgot to tell me where you'd leave it! It took a stroke of great luck that my friend, who's also my bike mechanic, happened to spot it right here. Isn't that crazy? Anyway, I kinda need my bike so I'm taking it back. Please accept this substitute until you can afford your own. Cheers!'

THE GREAT 'JP' MYSTERY
UK AND AROUND THE WORLD, 2013

It would be something of an understatement to say that Strava has been a big hit with cyclists since its release back in 2009. The website and mobile app that allows riders to plot and then record their routes via GPS and all sorts of other clever things has, frankly, been a runaway success, and by March 2015 Strava had over a million registered users. If you bought shares back in the day you could be the next Warren Buffet.

Strava's big selling point is the cycling community's thinly disguised competitiveness, allowing as it does professional and amateur riders alike to compete for the quickest times on prescribed routes, and cyclists jostle for coveted positions on the various virtual leader boards.

Which is why there was quite the kerfuffle when a mysterious Strava subscriber suddenly appeared on the scene in 2013, and proceeded to smash many of the existing best times that had been set on climbs surrounding London.

First the newbie tackled Box Hill in Surrey, which had featured in the Olympic road cycling race at London 2012, and destroyed the previous record set by pro rider Ian Bibby to become the new King of the Mountain. He then proceeded to try his luck on Toys Hill and Ide Hill in Kent, and once again he emerged as the fastest on two wheels.

Strava went into immediate meltdown. Who the hell did this new kid on the block think he or she was? No one knew, because, infuriatingly, the newcomer was only identified by the initials 'JP' on their Strava account, and so cycling's finest amateur sleuths set to work to try and unmask the elusive leader board interloper.

There were enough conspiracy theories to rival the assassination of John F. Kennedy. Some would-be DCIs suggested it was Tyler Hamilton, the disgraced former teammate of Lance Armstrong, while others were convinced it could be Armstrong himself, because the avatar on the aforementioned Strava account was a picture of the controversial American, and argued 'JP' could stand for Juan Pelota, the name of the café in his Austin bike shop.

Quite how someone as notorious but undeniably recognisable as Armstrong could get away with pedalling around the English countryside without being spotted was never adequately explained.

Other budding sleuths suggested the mystery cyclist was former British national hill-climb champion Jack Pullar, but the man himself denied it. Others argued the GPS data had in some way been tampered with but couldn't prove it, while some suggested the times had been set on a motorbike. The only thing people could actually agree on was a catchy moniker for the secret cyclist, dubbed as he was the 'Banksy of Strava'.

Since making his clandestine bow in 2013, the mystery rider has variously reappeared in Mallorca in August 2014, setting a new fastest time on the Sa Calobra hill segment, and again in early 2016, when he or she suddenly popped up in Australia and then Oman, once again to storm to the top of the climbing charts.

Intriguingly the setting of the last two times coincided with professional events in each country, suggesting the 'Banksy of Strava' was indeed a member of cycling's paid ranks, but we are not really any closer to unmasking the mystery figure.

'Who the **** is JP?' posted a rider nicknamed 'Durianrider' on the Strava website after his King of the Mountain time near Adelaide was expunged by Banksy. 'We're going to find out who this person is and bring them to Strava justice.'

THE FASHION POLICE

ENGLAND, 2013

Lycra is the Marmite of the sports clothing world. For some the material first known as Spandex and invented by boffins in the USA back in the late 1950s is an almost magical invention that has significantly enhanced athletic endeavour, while others consider it a sartorial abomination that can cause nausea and temporary blindness.

For those not enamoured by the world's stretchiest fabric, wearing Lycra is a crime against fashion, but this strange tale concerns a British cyclist who found himself on the wrong side of the law for *not* wearing impossibly tight shorts and a chest-hugging shirt.

The hapless rider to have his collar felt goes by the name of Tim Burton. A denizen of Bath, Tim was happily enjoying an innocent morning pedal in the West Country when he suddenly found himself confronted by Avon and Somerset Constabulary's finest, or PC Keith James as he's also known, who demanded to know what was going on.

Tim was stumped, what with not having broken any speed limits and, he was pretty sure, not having robbed any banks of late. The problem, PC James explained, was he was wearing jeans and T-shirt rather than standard issue Lycra, a sartorial statement, which lead the brilliant bobby to conclude Tim must have nicked the bike. An open and shut case surely.

The cuffs were out, only for Tim to patiently explain the £500 machine was indeed his property. PC James noted down the bike's frame number and ran a quick check. The police computer duly confirmed his story and a now somewhat red-faced copper reluctantly sent him on his way.

'Just got stopped by the police for "not wearing Lycra" but being on a road bike,' Tim tweeted after his brush with the law. "The PC said I wasn't dressed in appropriate gear to be riding my bike, so had I stolen it? I was clipped in. No scruffy trainers but clean(ish) SPD shoes. Maybe I didn't look hipster enough? It's fair enough. I'm not saying they were wrong. It's amusing that I've been stopped for no Lycra. Jeans and a tee are so last season.'

PC James was also evidently a devotee of social media, and hastily tried to put a spin on what had happened. 'Bike thefts are a priority for us in this area as we've had a number of garage and shed break-ins,' he said. 'I'm a cyclist myself and it was unusual to see an expensive bike being ridden by someone in non-cycling clothes and without a helmet. It soon became clear that Mr Burton was the genuine owner. I'm glad he's supportive of what we're doing to try to catch bike thieves.'

Profiling cyclists by their attire may not be the way forward, officer.

THE GREAT FALL OF CHINA

CHINA, 2015

We could have comfortably filled every single page of his book with terrible tales of cycling crashes and collisions. Incidences of two-wheeled wipeouts are commonplace and any cyclist who claims never to have hit the tarmac is doubtless suffering from amnesia – caused by the crash they can't now remember.

The finishing line of a race is one of cycling's most frequent scenes of carnage: all those riders pedalling at top speed, all jockeying recklessly for position, all focused on claiming victory. It's an accident waiting to happen, and of course all too often it does, as one wheel brushes disastrously against another or a rider is squeezed off the road.

This accidental anecdote from China and the Colorful Yunnan Gryffindor race (crazy name, crazy event) is, however, a little different and comes not as a result of over-competitiveness or the burning desire to win, but the abject absence of a sense of direction.

The race was reaching its climax, with a small lead group of riders pursued by the pack. The peloton then suddenly veered off the course onto a side road, but quickly realised the collective error of their ways, doubled back and rejoined the official route. Unfortunately the confusion caused by the brief detour had disorientated the leaders and although they had indeed got back on track, they were now heading in the wrong direction.

The race culminated in a stomach-churning pile-up on the finishing line as the former leaders renewed their acquaintance with the rest of the riders speeding in the opposite and correct direction. The two groups suddenly collided head-on in a bone-crunching, metal-bending coming together that made any Hollywood car crash scene look like a minor shunt.

A total of 17 riders were hospitalised as a result of the cataclysmic collision. At least 20 mangled bikes were consigned to the great two-wheeled graveyard in the sky, and inevitable questions about what the hell happened quickly followed.

Organisers of the Colorful Yunnan Gryffindor were quick to apologise and suggested the spectacular mishap had unfolded as a result of poor marshalling and errant signage during the race. They nervously promised to 'co-operate with relevant bodies and try their best in follow-up work', which given the totalitarian tendencies of the Chinese authorities was probably the least they could do.

HALF-INCHED IN AMSTERDAM

HOLLAND, 2015

The Netherlands has many and varied claims to fame. The Dutch are the tallest nation on the planet, with the average chap from Utrecht or Nijmegen standing at an imposing 6ft (1.8m), they're experts *par excellence* on all things tulips, and they're the country that gave the world Rembrandt and Vermeer.

On the other hand, Holland is a world leader in the illicit manufacture of ecstasy and LSD, and was also the birthplace of the *Big Brother* TV format. Not all good then.

The Dutch are also, it seems, some of Europe's most prolific bicycle pilferers. This is somewhat ironic, given the country's reputation as something of a cycling paradise, but the natives of Holland are apparently dab hands at pinching two-wheelers.

Our evidence for this outrageous statement comes from the curiously but aptly titled European Bike Stealing Championships, which were held in 2015. The brainchild of the online *We Love Cycling* magazine, the event was designed to raise awareness on the thorny issue of bicycle security, and saw the organisers set up shop in Amsterdam, Rome and Prague with an unlocked 'bait bike' to tempt would-be thieves. Hidden cameras lay in wait nearby and the bikes were rigged to explode in a harmless puff of red powder should any light-fingered local fall into the trap.

The results of the experiment were startling but hardly flattering from a Dutch perspective. The first two-wheeled theft in Amsterdam was carried out just 22 minutes after the bait was laid – perhaps not surprising for a city with a reported 45,000 incidences of bicycle pilfering per year – while it took a full 67 minutes for anyone in Rome to pluck up the courage and do a spot of purloining. If you want to head off on a city break safe in the knowledge you'll probably return home with all your valuables, Prague is evidently the place for you, as not one single attempt was made to pinch the bike in the Czech capital. Honest as the day is long, the Czechs.

Those caught out by the European Bike-Stealing Championships should count their blessings because bait bikes are not new, and an innocuous cloud of coloured powder ranks as a distinctly gentle punishment compared to what they dish out over the Atlantic.

One particularly cruel stunt staged in Los Angeles in 2016 saw two brothers electrify the handlebars of their bait bike and wait, camera poised, for a thief to hop on. The switch was only flipped when the bicycle bandit was in motion, causing predictably painful but hilarious crashes. Another painful prank involved a bike left tantalisingly unattended by a tree, but as any would-be criminal attempted to pedal off, a concealed rope attached to the bike's frame and tethered to the trunk would bring them to an abrupt and agonising halt.

A good sturdy lock is recommended as the best guard against having your wheels half-inched, but avoiding Amsterdam for your next cycling holiday comes a very close second.

STRONG-ARM TACTICS
BRAZIL, 2015

The cycling community's battle for dedicated metropolitan clearways has been a long but successful one, and today every self-respecting city boasts at least a few miles of tarmac that is forbidden ground to the internal combustion engine. The inconvenience and irritation caused when drivers selfishly clog cycling lanes with their cars is almost immeasurable. It's enough to turn even the most placid cyclist into a murderous psychopath, and who hasn't had their two-wheeled commute to work rudely interrupted by some idiot who's left their 4 x 4 in the wrong bloody place?

Such was the depressingly familiar dilemma faced by a resident of São Paulo in Brazil in 2015 when he found his prescribed route blocked by a motor, the rear of the offending car jutting out into the cycle lane. Our cyclist would have of course been forgiven for giving the vehicle a damn good kicking, but he decided to vent his frustrations in a rather more constructive way.

Luckily our cyclist was a muscular sort of chap and so he rolled up his sleeves (metaphorically at least – he was wearing a T-shirt), grabbed a firm hold on the rear bumper of what turned out to be a two-door Fiat Uno and began to lift it. In no time at all the back half of the motor was in the air, allowing our ripped rider to pivot the offending motor out of the cycle lane.

This thankfully was all caught on camera by a passing motorist – who obviously kept a safe distance just in case our anonymous muscle man fancied dead-lifting something else – and the cheers of appreciation from the other cyclists who had gathered to witness him victorious over the internal combustion engine were long and loud.

The video, entitled 'O homem mais forte do mundo' ('The strongest man in the world'), was quickly uploaded to YouTube – it's the law these days apparently – and within 24 short hours it had attracted over 600,000 views as people admired the Brazilian's muscular manoeuvrings. The identity of the unusual carjacker was sadly never made public, but in the weeks that followed, the motorists of São Paulo were uncharacteristically careful about where and how they parked their cars.

BICYCLING IN THE BUFF
ENGLAND, 2016

The south-west of England is a beautiful part of the country: all that unspoilt coastline, the unfeasibly charming country pubs and the rugged charms of Exmoor make it a phenomenally popular holiday destination. Throw in the delights of Babbacombe Model Village in Torquay, the Willows and Wetlands Visitor Centre near Taunton and not forgetting the Poldark Mine in Helston (other tourist attractions are available) and you've got a tourist Mecca on your hands.

It is, though, the gentle pace of West Country life that really draws the crowds and the escape it offers from the hustle and bustle of metropolitan life – people head west to get away from it all.

The peaceful idyll of the area, however, was bizarrely threatened in 2016 by a series of risqué bike rides that had Devon and Cornwall Police chasing a disrobed cyclist who liked to pedal under the cover of darkness. The hunt for the 'Naked Cycle Man' (let's call him NCM for short) was afoot.

The NCM's first appearance came in April in the city of Exeter. Technically he should have been dubbed Half-naked Cycle Man as he was wearing a hoodie, but he was nude from the waist down, and the locals certainly were unused to that sort of thing.

The emergency switchboard went into meltdown but the suspect got away under the cover of darkness, and all the police could do was to issue a description of a white male, aged in his late twenties or early thirties, with scruffy collar length hair and riding a dark-coloured bicycle, who was wanted for indecent exposure.

Devon's NCM kept a low profile for the next few months, but in the summer he resurfaced and this time there was no issue with false representation because he really wasn't wearing a stitch. The long arm of the law once again attempted to feel his collar but he wasn't actually wearing one, and once again his nocturnal pedalling conveyed him to safety.

'Exeter Response have been in pursuit of a naked cyclist who appears regularly at night,' tweeted Sergeant Harry Tangye, confirming the suspicion that going out and, you know, actually investigating things is like so 20th century. 'Are you the Naked Cycle Man? Do you know who he is?'

Unsurprisingly the incident line was not inundated with calls from the good folk of the West Country confessing to be our *au naturel* night-time cyclist, and the trail went cold, despite Devon and Cornwall Police's finest spending countless hours on social media asking if anyone could point them in the right direction.

At the time of going to press, the true identity of NCM remained a mystery, but some of Sergeant Tangye's Twitter followers speculated that since the end to his nocturnal, two-wheeled shenanigans coincided with the end of summer he might be 'mainly a seasonal problem'. Devon is bracing itself for a fresh flash of the flesh when things warm up a bit.

FIGHT THE FIREPOWER
USA, 2016

The American penchant for firearms is well documented. Our cousins across the pond are gaga for guns and from a cyclist's perspective, it may well add a certain frisson to one's daily pedal knowing that the driver of the Corvette in front may or may not be packing an AK47 in the glove compartment.

Motorists are, of course, capable of carrying significantly more firepower than their two-wheeled rivals, but size isn't everything, and more and more cyclists Stateside are fighting back when confronted by ballistic aggression on the streets of America.

In the New York City borough of Queens in 2016, for example, a cyclist was pedalling happily away when the driver of an SUV suddenly jumped out of his car and opened fire. The rider crashed his bike into a parked car after the surprise barrage, but quick as a flash was up on his feet, produced a pistol of his own and let off two shots at the hostile vehicle. The SUV sped off as the bullets flew, but our unhappy anonymous cyclist had made his point. Only in America.

The incident was captured on CCTV with no arrests being made, but the point is that cyclists in the USA have more reason than most to be wary, and there are almost too many tales to document of contretemps between cars and bikes climaxing in the irate car driver reaching for the Glock 43 they've got hidden in the trunk.

At times the poor besieged American cyclist cannot even trust the police. Back in New York and again in 2016, there were four couriers delivering food when one of their number was almost wiped out by an SUV in the cycle lane, and as the resulting 'disagreement' with the driver escalated, he pulled out a gun. His status as an off-duty copper mattered little; once again it was the cyclist staring down the barrel.

Such is the omnipresent danger that in 2015 one company began marketing the first ever cycling jersey for women featuring a concealed gun pocket. Produced by a company called *Concealed Carrie* and 'designed for the female shooter on the go', the product purportedly allowed ladies 'to conceal and carry their safety weapons whilst enjoying the great outdoors' and, should the fancy take them, alternatively be used to secretly carry pepper spray or a taser gun. The sales spiel concluded with the immortal tagline 'Firearms. Fashion. Fabulous'. Again, only in America.

DANGER, DANGER, HIGH VOLTAGE!

CROATIA, 2016

According to the esteemed Royal Society for the Prevention of Accidents, lightning hits the ground in Britain about 300,000 times every year. That's an awful lot of potentially fatal bolts of electricity for cyclists to successfully steer clear of, and the safety advice for those wishing to avoid instant death is not in truth entirely reassuring.

'Although there is no absolute protection from lightning,' admits the Society ominously, 'measures can be taken to reduce the risk of getting struck and the injury severity. Ideally, seek shelter inside a large building or a motor vehicle keeping away from, and getting out of wide, open spaces and exposed hilltops.

'If you are exposed to the elements with nowhere to shelter, make yourself as small a target as possible by crouching down with your feet together, hands on knees and your head tucked in. This technique keeps as much of you off the ground as possible.

'Be aware of objects that can conduct or attract lightning, for example, golf clubs, umbrellas, motorbikes, *bicycles*, wire fencing and rails. If you have a metal object that is not necessary for your safety, put it aside.'

Potentially not great news for cyclists, then, should the skies above dramatically darken, but fear not, because, as this story of one lucky Croatian rider proves, there is more than one way to avoid being burnt to a crisp at the roadside.

Our fortunate rider is 41-year-old Zoran Jorkovic, who found himself in the saddle outside his village of Petrovci when a storm suddenly rolled in and, thanks very much Royal Society for the Prevention of Accidents, he found himself rather bereft of a convenient shelter or indeed a car in which to hide. Poor Zoran was a sitting duck, and a lightning bolt soon struck his head with unerring and what should have been fatal accuracy.

Luckily for Zoran, he happened to be a man. More specifically, he was ultimately saved from certain death by his penis.

Concentrate now, here comes the science bit. The lightning bolt could not earth itself because Zoran was wearing thick rubber work boots. The bolt therefore should have passed through his body – in the process destroying his internal organs – but instead the surge of electricity travelled down through the cables of the headphones he was wearing and then safely earthed itself through his nether regions.

'I saw black clouds and flashes of light appear in the sky and thunder could be heard booming across the nearby fields,' Zoran later recalled. 'I tried to ride faster to get to shelter in time, but I was too late.'

He was not however completely unscathed by his highly charged experience, and somewhat dazed and confused, he was rescued by a passing motorist who rushed him to the nearest A&E department. 'We were shocked when we saw the man,' the driver said. 'He was sitting in the rain and steam was coming out of his body. The bicycle was next to him. We took him in our van and drove him to the hospital. Doctors were also amazed that he was alive.'

It is indeed a medical curiosity that Zoran survived, but the incident is even more noteworthy because it is the first time in recorded human history that a man's crown jewels had got him out of rather than into trouble.

TABLES TURNED ON DJ

ENGLAND, 2016

The bitter battle between cyclists and motorists has taken many curious twists over the years. It would be nice if the two seemingly diametrically opposed road-going factions could just get along, but hugs and kisses are currently in desperately short supply.

We have all sadly seen the all-too-frequent flare-ups between those on two wheels and those revving their 2-litre diesels. The common factor is the anger and indignation felt by both sides and, let's be honest, it's hardly unheard of for cyclists and motorists to vent their mutual frustrations with the occasional bout of fisticuffs.

Thankfully our next tale of the two tribes going to war is less violent and, depending on your point of view, either an example of impromptu genius or inexcusable theft. If you own a lot of Lycra and know what a sprocket is, you're probably going to be in the first camp.

The villain or motorist of this piece goes by the name of Nick Ahad, a DJ on BBC Radio Leeds, and a sometime script writer for *Emmerdale*, no less. Nick was enjoying a leisurely Sunday drive in his beloved Nissan in the scenic grounds – all 30,000 acres (12,141ha) of them – of Bolton Abbey in Yorkshire, when his motorised promenade was delayed by a cyclist who he claimed was 'zig-zagging' on the estate's roads and holding up traffic.

According to Nick, when he drew level with the erratic rider he politely enquired as to what exactly was the thinking behind his idiosyncratic style, but was met with a volley of abuse. The cyclist wasn't finished and proceeded to get off his bike and approach the open window of the driver's door. It was summer and miraculously it wasn't raining.

At this point, as we have discussed, driver versus cyclist confrontations have been known to get a bit, well, physical, but this time the rider renounced violence and instead leaned into the car, purloined Nick's keys and then sped off on his bike.

'There were lots of other cyclists on the road riding sensibly but he was weaving back and forth preventing cars from overtaking,' Nick told the local newspapers. 'As I finally managed to crawl past him I asked, "What do you think you're playing at?" I was really calm but he started shouting and swearing and, after pulling in front of my car, came back round to my driver's window. He didn't like the fact I wasn't rising to his anger, then, to my astonishment, he just leant in the car and grabbed my keys from the ignition. I didn't have time to react. It's not just the car key, my house keys were on there too. This real incident was a real nightmare.'

Nick's sudden immobility meant it was now him blocking traffic and one of Bolton Abbey's duty rangers had to be summoned to tow his Nissan out of the way. The pair then embarked on what unsurprisingly proved a fruitless search for the two-wheeled key snatcher – 30,000 acres, remember? – and after failing to get their man, the police were called. Nick, meanwhile, had to wait patiently for his family to show up and tow his motor home, the BBC apparently not paying enough for him to afford AA membership.

A description of a man riding a black and red bike and wearing a black and red helmet was duly circulated, but lawyers for Dennis the Menace were adamant their client was nowhere near Bolton Abbey on the day in question.

NOTTINGHAM'S
MYSTERY URBAN ARTIST
ENGLAND, 2016

'Graffiti's always been a temporary art form,' the elusive Bristolian artist Banksy once noted. 'You make your mark and then they scrub it off.' Unless of course it's one of Banksy's own creationsm, which can fetch north of £100,000 at auction. They're not so quick with the detergent, brushes and pressure washer then.

The popularity of Banksy's daubings has created much debate about the intrinsic value of graffiti or, of course, the lack of it. Does it enrich barren urban landscapes or is it simply mindless vandalism with no artistic merit? Should those with a penchant for spray paint be celebrated or summarily strung up?

Such questions were very much in the air in Nottingham in 2016, when an anonymous street painter began daubing the city's roads with what many considered very useful but unofficial advice for local cyclists.

The 'Phantom Aerosol', as he or she was dubbed, was evidently a big fan of two wheels and first got to work in March when they sprayed 'Unsafe Bike Lane' on a lane on which cyclists had injured themselves on tram tracks. Later the same month our clandestine sprayer marked another road with the legend 'Cyclist Priority' in a salutary warning to motorists, while the summer saw the secret urban artist daub another road as 'Door Lane', in reference to the number of riders poleaxed by errantly opened vehicular apertures.

Nottingham's beleaguered cyclists were amused by and appreciative of the Phantom's efforts in equal measure, but it's all about yin and yang, and those charged with the orderly running of the city's affairs were not amused one bit. 'We are arranging to have this graffiti removed as it is a potential distraction to drivers,' said a council spokesman, a social demographic not renowned for their sense of humour. 'The person or people behind this may think it's harmless fun but they are putting themselves and others at risk and placing unnecessary removal costs on local taxpayers. The county council does not encourage anyone to make a point in this fashion, which is essentially vandalism.'

The two-wheeled community quickly countered with the observation that drivers around Nottingham were no doubt similarly distracted by the plethora of pointless council signs warning of slow plant turning, fascinating changes in signal timing and the apocalyptic admission that the gap ahead has been closed but, like we said, councils are humourless places where ambition goes to die, and they weren't listening.

'The men' were duly dispatched to expunge the Phantom's work from Nottingham's streets, and the city's cyclists wailed. Banksy offered to pop over and do a satirical urban take on bicycling's eternal feud with the motoring industry and 'the man', but it never happened because he didn't include a name, address or contact number.

AN UNEXPECTED
TURN IN THE TOUR
WALES, 2016

Professional road racing is a young man's game. That's not ageism, it's just a fact. Chris Froome, for example, was 31 when he won the Tour de France in 2016, but once a rider reaches the big 3-0, the clock begins inexorably ticking, and it tells its own story that the oldest ever winner of the yellow jersey was Belgian Firmin Lambot, who was a positively wizened 36 years and four months old when he triumphed at the Tour back in 1922.

The dominance of the two-wheeled whippersnappers was, however, threatened during the 2016 Tour of Britain, when age thrust itself very firmly in front of beauty on the fourth stage of the race in North Wales.

Our champion of the dotage generation was 56-year-old father-of-two Roger Armstrong. Something of a veteran in cycling circles, Roger had plenty of experience in the saddle after undertaking charity rides from Land's End to John O'Groats, among others, but it was during the 2016 Tour that he really hit the headlines.

His specific claim to fame was the incredible five-minute lead he had built on a peloton that included Sir Bradley Wiggins and Mark Cavendish as the Tour made its way through the Principality from Denbigh to Builth Wells. Roger was so far in front Sir Bradley's sideburns were no more than a blur.

The crowd lining the course loved it as he rolled back the years, but sadly all was not as it seemed, as Roger was leading the race under false, albeit unwitting pretences.

'I decided to go out for my usual ride to the Horseshoe [near my village] but I didn't realise the Tour of Britain was passing through,' he explained. 'As I joined a road, I must have joined in between the first lot of police bikes. I was soon being passed by some early team cars and as I was heading down a stretch of road people were waving, clapping and taking photos.

'I had also chosen that day to ride in my Team GB Olympic kit and for one brief moment I was leading stage four. I thought I had better stop at the side of the road and wait but I wish now I had carried on down the road, milking the applause. I had pulled over as the main peloton came through. I was around five minutes ahead hence why I was able to cycle along.

'It was only when I saw some of the early team cars coming through it sank in so I pulled over and got talking to a couple of people and said I hadn't realised it was the Tour in this area. I must admit it was nice, if not a tad embarrassing, to see people clapping. It was my moment of cycling greatness.'

Unfortunately Roger's 'moment of greatness' wasn't exactly the PR boost some OAP cyclists were hoping for, rather proving as it did that riders of a certain age have a tendency to become disorientated, get lost and have to be enticed back home with the promise of a nice cup of tea and a piece of cake.

MARSUPIAL BREAST ENLARGEMENT

AUSTRALIA, 2016

By any measure Australia is a vast country. Really enormous. A grand total of 2,969,907 square miles (7,692,024 sq. km), to be precise, making it the sixth biggest nation on the planet, and if you're a cyclist down under you're spoilt for choice when it comes to selecting a scenic route away from congested city streets.

There are though, within the confines of the island, an estimated 60 million wild kangaroos. There should, you would have thought, be plenty of space for Australia's 20 million people and their muscular marsupial neighbours, but you'd be surprised how often *homo sapiens* and members of the Macropodidae family (that's Latin for 'large foot') come into disharmonious contact.

Just ask Sharon Heinrich, after she decided to take a recreational bike ride with a work pal in the lovely Clare Valley in South Australia. Sharon and friend Helen Slater were pedalling happily along until the pair came across a rocky outcrop and were suddenly assaulted by a roo with an attitude from above them.

'I've gone to ride past and I thought "He's cute" and he's just jumped [on] me and taken out the side of me,' Sharon said. 'As I'm falling, I felt him push off me and then he's flown to Helen and taken her out. He looked peaceful. He didn't look angry.'

Good at hiding their true feelings, those devious kangaroos. Sharon picked up three broken ribs in the incident, while Helen suffered concussion and whiplash but was thankfully able to get back into the saddle and pedal to the nearest phone to make the necessary emergency call. The pair were quickly rescued and taken off to hospital to be patched up.

You would of course be forgiven for thinking that Shazza and Helen would have become fully signed-up members of the 'We Hate Kangaroos' club after their painful experience, but Sharon was ultimately rather grateful to her marsupial assailant because the episode improbably saw her gain a bra size.

'When the surgeon saw me he said I was lucky to be alive,' she said. 'Kangaroos are solid muscle and incredibly powerful and my breast implants probably saved my life. They worked as air bags and have been ruptured by the ordeal. When he landed he went completely through me, if he had become caught in the bike the outcome would be a lot different.

'Santa brought me DDs in 2000, and it turns out they were 320 millilitres in size, but the surgeon this time has put in 400 millilitres so now they are bigger. Now I have an extra 80 each side. Australia can be a harsh country, so best to be safe now. I suppose I should be thanking the kangaroo.'

How exactly one goes about expressing gratitude to a pugnacious marsupial for accidentally amplifying one's assets is an etiquette dilemma for which not even *Debrett's* has an answer, but anyone wishing to do so could do worse than purchasing a box set of *Skippy the Bush Kangaroo*.

THE CAR PARK RODEO
USA, 2016

The cowboy is a powerful symbol of American pride, pioneering spirit and the ability to pull off wearing leather chaps without so much as a raised eyebrow. Without the cowboy, the West would never have been won, Clint Eastwood's film career would have never got off the ground and the entire population of Texas would have to find something else to wear on their heads. In fact the US of A remains so enamoured by its Wild West heritage that in 2005 the Senate declared the fourth Saturday of July each year the National Day of the American Cowboy.

It's easy, however, to think of the cowboy as part of a bygone era over on the other side of the Atlantic. After all, John Wayne's been dead since 1979 and there aren't so many horses that need wrangling these days, but our next tale proves that the cowboy spirit is undoubtedly alive and kicking.

The scene is thus. A woman has cycled to her local Walmart in the state of Oregon for a spot of shopping and has left her bike in the rack in the car park. When she emerged from the store, she saw a man brazenly riding away on her bike and after calling for help, gave chase to the thief on foot.

Unsurprisingly she didn't make much headway with her pursuit, but her cowboy in shining armour was nonetheless poised to intervene, in the shape of local rancher Robert Borba. He had heard her plaintive cries and just happened to have his horse and saddle with him, so he quickly leapt onto his trusty steed and set off after the criminal.

For the record, Robert was every inch the cowboy – denim shirt, jeans, big belt buckle, the hat, the complete works – and he and his horse were all over the bike thief like a rash. The only question now was how to bring him down, but Robert had excelled in all of his cowboy lessons, and simply reached for his lasso to halt his quarry. The robber suddenly found himself all tied up, and remained that way until the local sheriff turned up and arrested him.

'I seen this fella trying to get up to speed on a bicycle,' explained our Wild West vigilante after the successful chase. 'I wasn't going to catch him on foot. I just don't run very fast. I use a rope every day, that's how I make my living. If it catches cattle pretty good, it catches a bandit pretty good.'

Robert's exemplary rope work was the talk of the town.
'It was the best day of my life,' said one local who witnessed events unfold. 'I was laughing too hard to intervene. I've seen it all, but I've never seen anything like that in my entire life. The guy was just hanging back like "you ain't gonna steal no bike in front of me". This guy should be our next president.'

After 12 years of George Bush Senior and Junior in residence in the White House, many would argue that America has probably had enough presidential cowboys for the time being – although with Donald Trump now President-elect at the time of writing I don't think they are quite finished yet.

Cycling has encountered more enemies than any other form of exercise.

Louis Baudry de Saunier

BIBLIOGRAPHY

BOOKS

Cyclepedia: A Tour of Iconic Bicycle Designs, Michael Embacher & Paul Smith, Thames & Hudson, 2011

Cycling's 50 Craziest Stories, Les Woodland, McGann Publishing, 2010

Cycling's Greatest Misadventures, edited by Erich Schweikher & Paul Diamond, Casagrande Press, 2007

French Revolutions: Cycling the Tour de France, Tim Moore, Yellow Jersey, 2012

Guinness World Records 2017, Guinness World Records Limited, 2017

Muck, Sweat & Gears, Alan Anderson, Carlton Books Limited, 2011

The Bluffer's Guide to Cycling, Rob Ainsley, Bluffers, 2013

The History of Cycling in Fifty Bikes, Tom Ambrose, The History Press Limited, 2013

The Official Tour de France Records, Chris Sidwells, Carlton Publishing Group, 2014

The Story of the Tour de France, Bill McGann & Carol McGann, Dog Ear Publishing, 2006

The Splendid Book of the Bicycle, Daniel Tatarsky, Pavilion Books, 2016

WEBSITES

bicycling.about.com
www.bicycle-and-bikes.com
www.bikeradar.com
www.biography.com
www.brompton.co.uk
www.crazyguyonabike.com
www.cyclealert.com
www.cyclejumpers.com
www.cycletheearth.com
history.nasa.gov
www.ibike.org
www.myorangebrompton.com/
www.nbcnews.com
www.news-herald.com
www.oxfordtimes.co.uk
www.riaanmanser.com
www.topendsports.com

CYCLING HISTORY TIMELINE

1817 German Baron Karl von Drais patents his two-wheeled Laufmaschine (running machine) also known as the Draisine, Hobby Horse or Swift-Walker, that can be steered with handlebars.

1839 Scottish blacksmith Kirkpatrick MacMillan of Scotland adds cranks and treadmills to the rear axle of a two-wheeled vehicle, but gains only local interest as he did not think to patent his invention. He is now generally credited with the invention of the pedal bicycle.

1860s Pedals are added to the front wheel of a two-wheeled machine in separate adaptations by Frenchmen Pierre Michaux and Pierre Lallement, creating a bone-jarring machine called the velocipede or 'boneshaker'.

1868 Michaux forms a company with the Olivier brothers to mass-produce two-wheeled velocipedes.

1869 Solid rubber tyres replace iron velocipede tyres and the term 'bicycle' is first used. Jules Suriray patents ball bearings for wheel hubs.

1870s The unusually large high-wheel bicycle (penny-farthing or 'Ordinary') is developed.

1871 The Ariel, the first high-wheel Ordinary, is manufactured in Britain.

1874 James Starley designs the tangent-spoke wheel that has been used in the construction of almost all bikes ever since.

1876 The Ordinary or high-wheeler is first displayed in the USA.

1877 First American-made Ordinary is manufactured.

1878 The first portable bicycle made by William Grout.

1879 British designer Harry John Lawson patents a chain-driven bicycle.

1884 Thomas Stevens rides across the USA – from Oakland, California, to Boston, Massachusetts.

1885 John Kemp Starley introduces the Rover Safety Bicycle, which has a chain-driven rear wheel and wheels of similar size. The British Army scouts use bicycles for the first time.

1888 Inflatable tube tyres are invented by Scotsman John Boyd Dunlop.

1889 Daniel Stover and William Hance patent a bicycle with a back pedal brake.

1891 The Tandem Velocipede is patented by Henry Barr and Frank Peck.

1894 Annie Cohen Kopchovsky becomes the first woman to cycle around the world.

1896 William Reilly of Salford, England, patents a two-speed internal gear hub. The first Olympic bicycle race is held in Athens.

1898 Coaster brakes invented by American Willard M. Farrow.

1899 Charles M. 'Mile-a-Minute' Murphy of Queens, New York, USA, sets a bicycle speed record – 1 mile in 57.75 seconds.

1901 The first recumbent bicycles start to be sold (the Brown Recumbent Bicycle).

1903 The first Tour de France takes place, with six stages with an average length of over 249 miles (400km). Bicycle mechanics Wilbur and Orville Wright fly 120ft (36.6m) in the first successful airplane.

1905 Frenchman Paul de Vivie invents a two-speed rear derailleur gear.

1920 The first children's bikes are produced in the USA.

1930 Italian racing cyclist Tullio Campagnolo invents the first bicycle hub quick release.

1937 Derailleur gears are introduced to the Tour de France – riders can select new gears without changing wheels.

1970 Mountain bikes are invented by Charlie Kelly, Gary Fisher and Tom Ritchey.

1972 Bicycles outsell cars in the USA (13 million to 11 million); bicycle thefts account for 17 per cent of all theft in the USA.

1974 The first organised BMX (Bicycle Motocross) race is held.

1981 The Specialized Stumpjumper becomes the first mass-produced mountain bike.

1984 The road race becomes the first women's cycling event at the Olympics.

1990–92 Australia passes the first laws to make the wearing of bicycle helmets compulsory.

1993 Electric derailleur gears introduced by Mavic.

1996 Mountain biking introduced as an Olympic sport in Atlanta, USA.

1999 Lance Armstrong wins the Tour de France for the first time.

2005 Lance Armstrong wins the Tour de France for the seventh time.

2008 BMX biking appears as an Olympic sport for the first time in Beijing.

2012 Sir Chris Hoy wins his sixth cycling Olympic gold medal at the London Olympics.

2012 Lance Armstrong is stripped of his Tour de France victories following a doping scandal.

2016 Jason Kenny wins his sixth cycling Olympic gold medal.

OTHER TITLES IN

THE STRANGEST® SERIES

The *Strangest* series has been delighting and enthralling readers for decades with weird, exotic, spooky and baffling tales of the absurd, ridiculous and the bizarre. This range of fascinating books – from Football to London, Rugby to Law and many subjects in between – details the very curious history of each one's funniest, oddest and most compelling characters, locations and events.

9781910232910   9781910232866

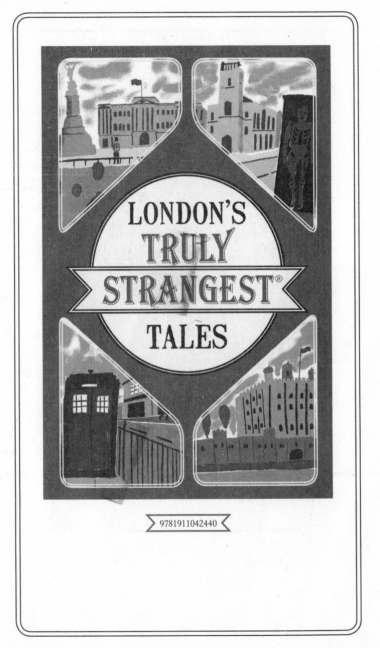

LONDON'S
TRULY
STRANGEST®
TALES

9781911042440

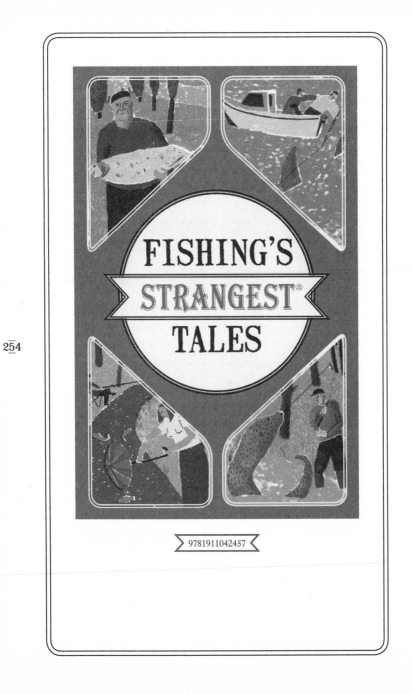

9781911042457

SAILING'S STRANGEST TALES
9781911042259

SHAKESPEARE'S STRANGEST TALES
9781910232903

253

TEACHERS' STRANGEST TALES
9781910232989

TENNIS'S STRANGEST MATCHES
9781910232958

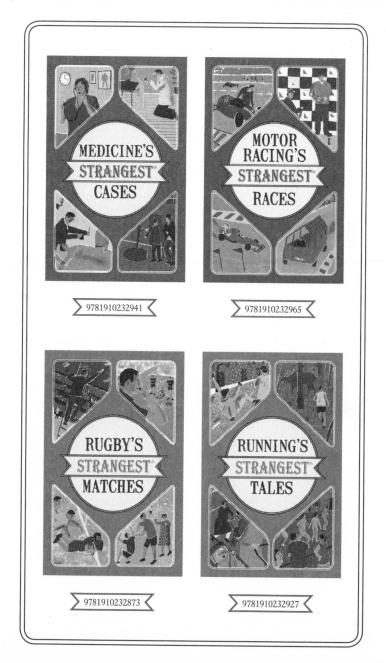

MEDICINE'S STRANGEST CASES

9781910232941

MOTOR RACING'S STRANGEST RACES

9781910232965

RUGBY'S STRANGEST MATCHES

9781910232873

RUNNING'S STRANGEST TALES

9781910232927

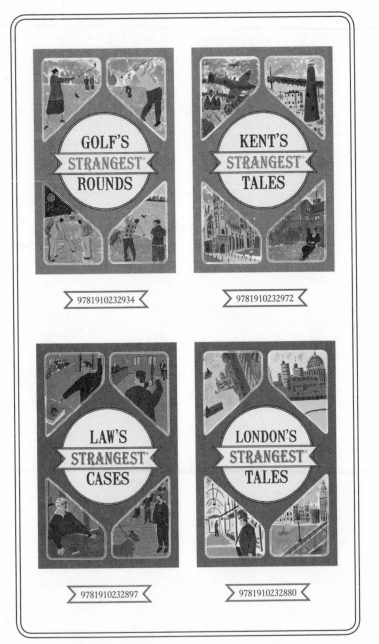

GOLF'S STRANGEST ROUNDS

9781910232934

KENT'S STRANGEST TALES

9781910232972

LAW'S STRANGEST CASES

9781910232897

LONDON'S STRANGEST TALES

9781910232880